D0475531

THE
CIVIL WAR
IN COLOR

THE
CIVIL WAR
IN COLOR

A PHOTOGRAPHIC
REENACTMENT
OF THE WAR
BETWEEN THE STATES

JOHN C. GUNTZELMAN

FOREWORD BY BOB ZELLER,

STERLING
New York

STERLING
New York

An Imprint of Sterling Publishing
387 Park Avenue South
New York, NY 10016

STERLING and the distinctive Sterling logo are registered trademarks of Sterling Publishing Co., Inc.

© 2012 by John Guntzelman
See picture credits on page 256 for image copyright

All rights reserved. No part of this publication may be reproduced, stored in a retrieval system,
or transmitted, in any form or by any means, electronic, mechanical, photocopying,
recording, or otherwise, without prior written permission from the publisher.

ISBN 978-1-4027-9081-2
ISBN 978-1-4549-0496-0 (book club)

Distributed in Canada by Sterling Publishing
c/o Canadian Manda Group, 165 Dufferin Street
Toronto, Ontario, Canada M6K 3H6
Distributed in the United Kingdom by GMC Distribution Services
Castle Place, 166 High Street, Lewes, East Sussex, England BN7 1XU
Distributed in Australia by Capricorn Link (Australia) Pty. Ltd.
P.O. Box 704, Windsor, NSW 2756, Australia

Book design, layout, and editorial services: gonzalez defino, ny/gonzalezdefino.com

For information about custom editions, special sales, and premium and corporate purchases,
please contact Sterling Special Sales at 800-805-5489 or specialsales@sterlingpublishing.com.

Manufactured in China

4 6 8 10 9 7 5

www.sterlingpublishing.com

For my lovely wife, Dixie, who encourages me in my every endeavor . . .
for my brother, Dan, who has proven time and again that goals
you really want to achieve are within your reach . . .
and for the intrepid photographers of the American Civil War,
who would have done it this way if they could have.

CONTENTS

FOREWORD
by Bob Zeller

In hand-coloring some of the most iconic images of the Civil War, artist John Guntzelman is following a tradition not only from the war itself, but one that stretches back almost to the invention of practical photography more than two decades earlier. Let there be no debate here, no hand-wringing among traditionalists as with the oft-debated practice of colorizing black-and-white movies. The application of color to the black-and-white or sepia-toned images of the Civil War era was a common and popular practice among the photographers themselves.

The nineteenth century was a world ablaze with color, from the bright blues and greens and reds of fancy women's dresses, to the rainbows of color in elaborate flower gardens, to even the ever-distinctive, yellow-painted "omnibuses" that taxied New Yorkers up and down Broadway during the Civil War.

Almost as soon as the first daguerreotype photograph appeared on display in New York City on December 20, 1839, captivating the country with the magical perfection of its "sun painting," photographers began to add color.

The most common method was to apply color to the silver-plated daguerreotype photograph with a finely pointed camel-hair brush, applying dry powdered pigment directly to the polished silver surface, which was made slightly tacky by a thin coating of a solution of isinglass.

"Diamonds were made to shine by digging into the surface of the plate with the sharp point of an awl, laying bare a point of silver," writes photo historian Beaumont Newhall. "Jewelry was painted gold."[1]

Many Civil War-era tinting artists took pains to produce accurate and precisely executed colorized images, such as the unknown artist who added color to this Gardner photograph of a group at the secret intelligence service headquarters, Army of the Potomac, at Antietam. (1862. Alexander Gardner, photographer.)

A daguerreotype colorist, holding his brush and sitting with his equipment, poses in the mid-1850s for his own daguerreotype, which, curiously, was not tinted. (Date and photographer unknown.)

This 1850s daguerreotype tinting kit is the same type of kit visible in the daguerreotype of the colorist.

The purists howled back then, too. Some daguerreian artists believed that nothing could surpass the gleaming beauty and elegance of a perfectly exposed daguerreotype.[2] In April 1854, the trade magazine *Photographic Art Journal* conceded that many daguerreian photographers hand-colored their images, but argued that "they must in their own minds condemn it, as they know that they are working to please the bad tastes of the community and not their own."[3]

Yet, only a modest percentage of daguerreotypes were colored. The demand was high enough, however, that any daguerreian artist mindful of good business practices had better offer the option. Some daguerreian artists took the next step and began experimenting to see if they could capture natural colors on their daguerreotype plates.

In late 1850 and early 1851, the burgeoning photography industry was electrified and tantalized with the news that an upstate New York daguerreian artist, the Rev. Levi L. Hill, was claiming that he had produced daguerreotypes in natural colors, which he named "hillotypes."

"For instance, we can produce *blue, red violet,* and *orange* on one plate, at one and the same time. We can, also, produce a landscape, with these colors beautifully developed. . . . The great problem is solved," Hill wrote in November 1850. "In a short time it will be furnished to all who are willing to pay a moderate price for it."[4]

The excitement was keen within the vast community of American daguerreian artists, especially when other daguerreian artists traveled to Hill's studio and reported that, yes, they had seen color plates. The inventor Samuel F. B. Morse himself—the man largely responsible for introducing the daguerreotype to the United States—visited Hill, saw his work, and declared, "I have no doubt whatever of the reality of his discovery."[5] Across America, thousands of daguerreian photographers told tens of thousands of customers, "Soon we will offer daguerreotypes in natural colors!"

It never happened. Hill was a strange character; he refused to leave his studio or allow his color images to be displayed. He was still working on the process, he said. Until he was finished, "all will be kept a profound secret."[6]

Other artists visited; this time he showed them nothing. As time passed, the controversy increased. Year after year, acrimony and accusations filled the pages of photographic journals. Hill offered a litany of excuses for the delays, saying at one point that "invisible goblins" had stymied him.[7]

In 1855, when Hill finally published his formula for making hillotypes, it was largely ignored. New photographic processes were proliferating, and the archaic language that Hill used to describe his formula was all but undecipherable. By the time he died in 1865, the question of whether or not he had taken color photographs was all but forgotten.

With the dream of photographs in natural color still a dream, photographers settled back into the custom of using tinting artists to apply color. That did not change until the arrival of new photographic processes in the 1950s.

The daguerreotype was gradually rendered obsolete in the mid-1850s, replaced by images on glass (ambrotypes) and metal (tintypes). In the late 1850s, the advent of glass-plate negatives, which could be used to make limitless paper prints, created a whole new arm of the photographic industry almost overnight. For the first time, photographers could mass market their images.

Photographers produced large-sized prints, of course, but the most popular paper photographs were "carte de visite" card photographs and stereographs (also known as stereo views) that had side-by-side images mounted on a rectangular card for 3-D viewing. The photographic paper used back then—albumen paper—yielded a brownish, sepia-toned print that did not have the exquisite tones of a daguerreotype plate, so no hand-wringing accompanied the use of applied color on albumen prints. Still, most albumen photographs were left uncolored, based on this author's observation that fewer than 10 percent of vintage stereo views offered for sale at today's antique photo markets are colored, and even fewer card photographic portraits.

The hand-tinting of stereo views often enhanced the sense of reality conveyed by the photograph, but could just as easily detract if not applied with judicious skill.

E. & H. T. Anthony & Co. was the nation's largest seller of stereo views during the Civil War, and the artists they employed to apply color to their stereo views of the Civil War appear to have been instructed to follow a set pattern of painting the sky blue and the horizon orange. This custom is seen in most tinted Anthony war views that survive today. In most cases, it added a pleasingly colored background to an otherwise blank sky, since clouds almost never appear in the skies of Civil War photographic exposures. But the blue-and-orange sky tint was used, at least sometimes, in far less appropriate situations, such as in the background sky of some of the Anthony Company's *Broadway on a Rainy Day* series of popular stop-action stereographs. The weird juxtaposition of a blue sky in the background and a rain-soaked scene in the foreground, with pedestrians carrying umbrellas, created a sense of unreality.

In the spring of 1865, the Anthony Company issued its massive *War for the Union* series of 1,120 Civil War stereo photographs. This series appears to have sold quite well, contrary to the commonly held notion that Civil War photos had become unpopular by the end of the war.

In 1867, the Anthony Company charged $5.00 a dozen for the *War for the Union* stereo views, or 42 cents each, significantly more than the 25 cents charged for a carte de visite in 1862. In today's dollars, $5.00 equates to $77.00, or $6.42 each per view. For colored views, though, the Anthony Company charged $7.00 per dozen, or $8.98 each in today's dollars.[8]

Perhaps the demand for the more expensive hand-colored views did not meet expectations, because two years later, war views still cost $5.00 a dozen, but for colored views, the price was slashed a full dollar to $6.00 a dozen.[9]

Despite the fact that this E. & H. T. Anthony & Co. stereo view shows Broadway in New York City on a rainy day, the tinting artist has followed an Anthony custom by coloring the sky blue and the horizon orange. (ca. 1860. E. & H. T. Anthony & Co., publisher.)

The war's most prolific documentary photographer was Alexander Gardner, who worked for Mathew Brady before going on his own in 1863. Gardner produced more than 1,200 stereo views and almost 950 large-plate photographs during the war, offering both uncolored and colorized versions.

Yet, of those tinted Gardner views encountered today, very few could be deemed as having even moderately acceptable quality. Although a few excellent examples do exist, the colors on extant Gardner tinted views generally are applied far too thickly, and rather than enhancing the photographic features of the image, the paint usually overshadows it, eliminating the precise features and details that make a photograph a photograph. In some cases, the tinting is so garish, the features of the photograph are virtually unrecognizable.

In one very distinctive way, however, the tinting on some of Gardner's stereo photographs tells another story that speaks to the emotional impact of his most gruesome images. Gardner's photographs of the dead soldiers on the Antietam battlefield were the first images of American war dead, and they were a sensation when first display at Brady's New York gallery just a few weeks after the battle of September 17, 1862.

"Let him who wishes to know what war is look at this series of illustrations," wrote Oliver Wendell Holmes, the great nineteenth-century essayist who also co-invented the practical, hand-held stereo viewer.[10]

"Mr. Brady has done something to bring home to us the terrible reality and earnestness of war," reported the *New York Times* on October 20, 1862.[11]

After leaving Brady's employ and establishing his own gallery in Washington, D.C., Gardner continued selling the Antietam photographs with his own label throughout the war. And if the images of the bloated dead—frozen by rigor mortis in horrific positions—were not graphic enough, Gardner was more than willing to have his tinting artists enhance the effect by painting some red blood into the scene.

One of the most distinctive vintage Gardner Antietam stereo views in my collection is a garishly tinted view in poor condition showing dead Confederates along the Hagerstown Pike. Blood is painted onto both bodies. But it is the application of red paint on the corpse on the right that is particularly distinctive. The blood trail starts as trickle at the right side of the soldier's mouth, and it spreads down his chin and neck into an ever-widening patch around his upper chest.

Both halves of the stereo view are painted the same, which establishes that this pattern was not random. Could Gardner himself—the photographer who viewed the scene with his own eyes—have instructed the artists on how and where to add the blood? Perhaps he told the artists: "This is what I saw. Paint it this way."

The original negative of this view still exists today at the Library of Congress, and a careful examination of the high-resolution digital version of the image shows no evidence of bloodstains in the areas that were painted red on the bodies. Still, it is likely that the instructions to add blood, often lots of it, came directly from the man who made the original photographs. And the tendency to add a good bit of it

Entered according to Act of Congress, in the year 1863, by Alex. Gardner, in the Clerk's Office of the District Court of the District of Columbia.

Vintage, original, hand-tinted Civil War stereo views sold by Gardner's Gallery in Washington, D.C. were often badly painted, such as this almost unrecognizable image of Little Round Top at Gettysburg. (1863. Alexander Gardner, photographer.)

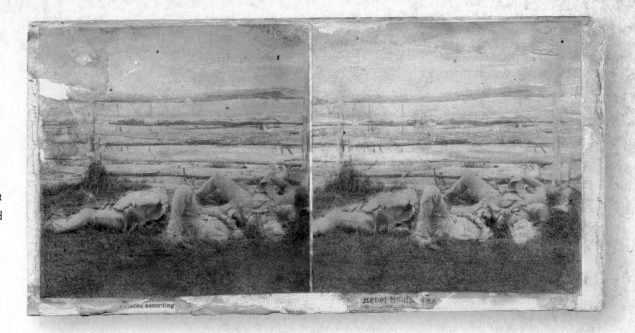

As if Gardner's views of the dead on the Antietam battlefield were not gruesome enough, his coloring artists added red paint for blood. This hand-colored image included a specific blood pattern on the center figure that started with a trickle at the mouth and ended in a pool on the chest. (1862. Alexander Gardner, photographer.)

could well have been born in the memories of those gruesome sights Gardner photographed.

The black-and-white world gradually faded with the introduction of color photographic processes in the last half of the nineteenth century. That transition was completed in the 1980s when newspapers began publishing color photographs routinely, and the black-and-white format became the domain of artists and specialists.

The world of color photography—the dream of so many daguerreian artists—finally came true. And the mystery of Levi L. Hill's work remained just that—a mystery—until 1980, when photo historian Wm. B. Becker revealed that after a tip from fellow historian Joel Snyder of the University of Chicago, he had found Hill's original "hillotype" plates buried and forgotten in the deep recesses of the Smithsonian Institution, and that they did, indeed, appear to have some natural color.[12]

And then, in 1984, after several years of painstaking study and experimentation, photography professor Joseph Boudreau succeeded in deciphering Hill's arcane published formula and made modern "hillotype" plates that contain natural colors. The mystery had finally been solved; Hill was not a fraud after all.

Thus, perhaps but for fate, the Civil War was photographed only in black and white. The grand panoply of color during the conflict—the vivid blues of the Union uniforms, the bright gold flourishes on the muted gray Confederate uniforms, the muddy browns of the water-filled trenches of Petersburg—was absent to the eye except when applied by the artist's brush.

And so it is with *The Civil War in Color*, with the images rendered in the full spectrum of color by the precision of artist John Guntzelman. In these pages, the war comes alive, allowing us to see the photographs of the conflict with a keener sense of how these scenes actually appeared. ❖

NOTES
1. Beaumont Newhall, *The Daguerreotype in America* (New York: Dover Publications, 1976), 96.
2. The daguerreotype photograph was an image on a polished, silver-surfaced copper plate that was invented by the Frenchman Louis Jacques Mande Daguerre and introduced to the world in 1839.
3. Newhall, *The Daguerreotype in America*, 96.
4. Ibid., 97.
5. Ibid.
6. Ibid., 98.
7. Ibid., 103.
8. *1867 New Catalogue of Stereoscopes and Views* (New York: E. & H.T. Anthony & Co.), 63 and *Catalogue of Card Photographs*, Nov. 1862 (New York: E. & H. T. Anthony & Co.), 13. Copies in author's collection.
9. *1867 New Catalogue of Stereoscopes and Views* (New York: E. & H.T. Anthony & Co.), 28. Copy in author's collection.
10. Oliver Wendell Holmes, "Doings of the Sunbeam," *Atlantic Monthly*, July 1863, 11.
11. "Brady's Photographs: Pictures of the Dead at Antietam," *New York Times*, October 20, 1862.
12. Wm. B. Becker, "Are These the World's First Color Photographs?" *American Heritage*, June–July 1980, 4–7; and "Inventive Genius or Ingenious Fraud?—The Enduring Mystery of Levi L. Hill," *Camera Arts*, January–February 1981, 28. Subsequent analysis by the Smithsonian Institution has determined that some hillotype plates contain both natural color and applied color.

INTRODUCTION

April 12, 2011 marked the one hundred and fiftieth anniversary of the bombardment of Fort Sumter— the beginning of the American Civil War. Those one hundred and fifty years have seen the rise of great cities, the quadrupling of world population, and unbelievable developments in technology. Considering what we now accept as commonplace, it is no wonder then that the Civil War era seems lost in the murky dust of time. One hundred and fifty years, though, is but the span of two average lifetimes and truly not that far in the past. However, photography was only in its infancy then, and the faded, scratched images from that time seem impossibly dated. They possess an archaic quality that seems to defy the notion that they were ever real moments in time, even though that is exactly what they are. Motion pictures and battle-reenactment photographs have a far more "real" appearance to our present-day eyes than actual photos from the late nineteenth century, yet these photos are our only accurate and real connection to that bygone era.

Photography during the Civil War was a daunting task. A photographer and his assistant would arrive at a site in their wagon and set up a tent to use as a darkroom. While the photographer placed his camera in the best location to create his picture, his assistant would coat a glass plate with collodion, a sticky, syrupy adhesive, and then place the glass into a silver nitrate solution to make it sensitive to light. While still wet, the plate was put into a light-tight carrier, taken to the camera, and placed in it. It was exposed for several seconds, replaced in the light-tight carrier, removed from the camera, and taken back to the tent for developing. The glass plates generally needed a few seconds of exposure to light, which required the subjects to remain absolutely still during the exposure time, so as not to be blurred in the final photo. Because of that, there are very few action shots of the Civil War, and it is quite common to see a head, a hand, or an entire person blurred in a photograph because they moved during the interval of exposure. With all of those limitations it is little wonder the pictures seem very dated.

Although the process was labor intensive and often tedious for photographers, it was a novel experience for most of the subjects—an occasion causing many to don their best clothes and outfit themselves as if going to an event. People were posed in groupings that look staged to our modern eyes, and even battlefield scenes were often posed in ways that allowed the subjects to remain stationary to accommodate the requirements of early photography.

While primitive photographs of earlier conflicts do exist from the Mexican-American War (1846–48) and the Crimean War (1853–56), the American Civil War became the first large-scale military endeavor to be thoroughly covered by photographers. Mathew Brady is probably the best known, but he had many colleagues, intrepid photographers who roamed battlefields both North and South, recording the war for posterity. While these photographs appear somewhat archaic in composition and execution, the large size of the glass-plate negatives allowed photographers to produce incredibly detailed images.

In 1911, the year that marked the fiftieth anniversary of the beginning of the Civil War, a truly remarkable book titled *The Photographic History of the Civil War in Ten Volumes* was published to commemorate the event. That very successful book is long since out of print, but copies of the work are still available, usually costing between five hundred and one thousand dollars for the complete set. A rather poor-quality scan of it can be found on the Internet. That massive work was astounding because it was so thoroughly comprehensive and dedicated to the subject matter. Now, one hundred years after that work, and one hundred and fifty years after the war itself, *The Civil War in Color* presents some of the most outstanding and remarkable of these actual Civil War photographs and, with painstaking use of modern technology, presents them as they have never been seen before—in color.

Concerns have been voiced when motion pictures have been colorized. A movie, however, is an artistic work of fiction often made in black and white as a creative choice. These Civil

A Civil War photographer and his portable darkroom wagon at a signal tower in Bermuda Hundred, Virginia. See entire image on page 109. (1864. Photographer unknown.)

War photographs are something else altogether—they depict real events and were created under real conditions. While they are most definitely works of art, they are first and foremost a graphic record of those events and times.

The most important benefit, then, of colorizing these historic photos is that they become far more relevant and realistic to modern eyes. They are no longer merely dusty images of an even dustier past; the addition of color makes the places real, the events comprehensible, and the people understandable. In short, the use of color brings these remarkable photos to life. When we look into the faces of long-gone men, women, and children, we see the common link of humanity that connects us all.

I have taken extreme care to restore the images to their original condition. In all cases, scratches and other imperfections in the original pictures have been carefully minimized to clean them up. In a few photographs, cracked glass plates have been painstakingly put back together so as not to detract from the subject matter. I used best-guess choices as well as referencing period paintings and researching existing uniforms and other paraphernalia to arrive at appropriate color choices. Nothing has been added to these priceless photos, nor have they been changed in any way; they are just as they were when they were exposed one hundred-and-fifty years ago, except for the addition of color.

It is through the courtesy of the U.S. Library of Congress and their dedicated historians and technicians that these priceless photographs are still available in such wonderful condition. Over time, thousands of original black-and-white negatives and prints from various Civil War collections have been located, purchased, collated, preserved, copied, and scanned so as to be safeguarded for future generations.

At the end of each chapter I have included a few of the original black-and-white photographs that can be directly compared with the fully colorized versions. Such a comparison immediately reveals the vibrant reality that color brings to these photos. While colorizing these images, I was astounded by the incredible detail contained in the original negatives. In some cases I have included enlargements of features not easily recognized or readily apparent in the entire photo. You'll notice the details of shoes, clothing, buildings, everyday items, and, especially, faces, which reveal the sameness of people then as they are now. Skies were as blue, trees were as green, and people were just as diverse.

The Civil War in Color is not specifically a history book, but rather a visual tour of what life was like for the people who lived through one of the greatest periods of turbulence in the American experience, one that threatened to rip the United States asunder a century and a half ago. These photos are no longer just old pictures, but rather very real moments in time from our collective past, frozen forever in color. ❖

A NOTE ON COLORIZING

The mid-1860s were every bit as vibrant and colorful a world as ours is today, but that era has long been hidden behind a veil of gray imposed by the limitations of photography at that time. Though limiting, the art and alchemy of photography had at least progressed to a workable level fully capable of recording the American Civil War, which consequently became the first major war to be thoroughly captured by the camera. Technical constraints dictated that the work was cumbersome and time consuming under the best circumstances, and far more so when taking photographs on battlefield locations under strenuous and potentially dangerous conditions. Many fearless photographers ignored these obstacles and instead looked upon them as challenges. Those challenges were triumphantly overcome by the numerous Civil War photographers whose body of work has left us a stunning and remarkable record of the people and places of that time. The only difficulty they could not overcome is that the resulting photographs were incapable of capturing color. That one limitation removes much of the impact and reality of the photographs for many, if not most, modern-day viewers. At the time, some Civil War photographs were tinted or patiently hand-colored, but the

results were uneven and the numbers few due to the laborious and time-consuming task of hand-coloring. Portraits were more often hand-tinted because the detail was simpler than in wider battlefield views or group shots. Dyes, watercolor, oil paints, crayons, and pastels were all used by artists to selectively add color to black-and-white photographic prints. The more transparent of these materials were usually the most effective because they allowed the photographic detail to be readily seen under the color overlay. The work done on the best hand-colored photos was rather good quality when one considers the labor involved and the limited color palette available to an artist trying to achieve a relatively accurate color rendition.

When I chose to bring color to this long-lost world, I knew that doing so would instantly make the resulting images far more compelling and believable to modern viewers. I also appreciated the great responsibility of doing so in a realistic and honorable manner so as to respect the historical importance and significance of these priceless images. A huge amount of research was required to answer the hundreds of questions about the almost endless details of the subjects. What color were Abraham Lincoln's eyes? What was the correct hair color for Ulysses S. Grant, Robert E. Lee, George Armstrong Custer? Were some of the cannons made from cast bronze instead of cast iron, which would then dictate a different color? Were ladies' clothing colors from that time brilliant or more muted? What did Zouave uniforms look like? My forty-plus years as a professional cinematographer and director of photography allowed me to view the original photographs with a trained professional eye and visualize a full range of appropriate colors and how they would interplay in the final colorized image. Obviously there was sizeable latitude allowed for color interpretation, but I still needed actual guidance as a realistic and believable departure point. Ladies' garments, for instance, permitted a fair amount of leeway in color choices; uniforms, both North and South, did not. Exterior building colors had to be appropriate for the era. The colors

Photographer James F. Gibson took this detailed photograph of wounded Union soldiers being tended to at a makeshift field hospital in Savage's Station, Virginia, during the Peninsula Campaign, shown in three versions here: the original black-and-white, the contemporary hand-colored, and my colorized version. Note how in the hand-colored version the artist has taken creative license by adding "blood" to some of the wounded, while in actuality, no blood is visible on the original black-and-white image. (June 30, 1862. James F. Gibson, photographer.)

Detail of colorized photograph of Lieutenant George Armstrong Custer during the Peninsula Campaign in Virginia. His hair color is based on deductive research. See entire image on page 72. (1862. Photographer unknown.)

Brigadier General Rufus Ingalls (seated in center chair), the chief quartermaster for the Army of the Potomac, with a group at City Point, Virginia. Ladies' clothing allowed for more leeway in the colorization process than military uniforms. See entire image on pages 132-133. (May 1865. Photographer unknown.)

of illustrations painted on the sides of drummer boys' drums had to match those of actual drums from the war. Searches on the Internet—literally hundreds of searches—ultimately made this huge undertaking a realistic proposition. I was able to visit many modern sutler companies, which make uniforms, hats, guns, and thousands of other items used by present-day reenactors, who are absolute fanatics for authenticity in materials and colors. I also went to many historic sites dedicated to preserving the memory of the war from essentially every standpoint in order to view actual uniforms, flags, and implements preserved from the war. Visiting sites dedicated to Civil War arms and armaments allowed me to get a better understanding of the technology of the era. After literally hundreds of such searches, I was able to lock down an honest feeling for most of the technical details of the war. However, personal details were not quite as straightforward. While searching for descriptions of hair and eye colors of principal figures, I found that many discrepancies exist. One description might state that Lincoln's eyes were gray and another might say black; one source might say that Custer's hair was light brown while another called it reddish blonde. In such cases I continued investigating until I found a majority agreement and settled on that.

The colorizing technology utilizes a transparent color overlay, which fully retains the contrast and brightness ranges of the original black-and-white image and in no way modifies it. Thus, a color assigned to, let's say, a shirt, will be appropriately lighter or darker in the folds of the material. For continuity purposes, once I arrived at appropriate color values for uniforms and other repetitive items, I was able to duplicate those color values from picture to picture. Because of my background in cinematography, I was able to devise methods of dealing with extremely complicated portions of images, such as trees against sky. My approach allowed me to tint the trees green and

This hand-colored portrait of an unidentified Union soldier astride his horse presented more details for the artist to colorize than more typical close-up portraits. (1861-65. Photographer unknown.)

Blue sky is visible through the green trees in this detail of blacksmiths shoeing horses at the headquarters of the Army of the Potomac at Antietam, Maryland, in my new colorized image. See entire colorized photograph on page 90. (September 1862. Alexander Gardner, photographer.)

A close-up of my colorized version of President Lincoln and General George B. McClellan in the general's tent at Sharpsburg, Maryland. See entire colorized photograph on page 198. (October 3, 1862. Alexander Gardner, photographer.)

the visible sky blue without having to colorize each branch or individual bundles of leaves—an impossible task!

Just how well a black-and-white photograph's inherent brightness and contrast ranges controlled the color overlay was brought home to me when colorizing the portrait of Abraham Lincoln found on page 24. I worked with the portrait for a long while, and in each attempt his skin color seemed ruddy and almost tanned. I then decided to try an online search for "Lincoln's complexion." Such an Internet search originally seemed rather far-fetched to me, but here are some of the quotes I found:

- William Herndon, Lincoln's friend and law partner for many years, said "his complexion was very dark, his skin yellow, shriveled and leathery."

- Horace White, city editor of the *Chicago Evening Journal* described Lincoln as "raw boned, with a complexion of leather," and again "with a ruddy complexion."

- Poet Walt Whitman mentioned Lincoln's "dark brown complexion."

- Noah Brooks, a friend and frequent to the White House as well as a journalist, called Lincoln's countenance "sallow."

These quotes are but a few of those I found, which suggest that my color values, as interpreted by the black-and-white contrast and brightness ranges of the original photographs, may be closer to reality than anyone can ever know.

The Civil War in Color began as a casual conversation between my wife and me while vacationing in Maui in 2007. At the time she was reading *Blood, Tears, and Glory*, a most interesting book about the war by James Bissland. I knew there is always a great amount of interest in the Civil War and the upcoming sesquicentennial would generate even more interest. One thing led to another, and the idea of this book was born. After our vacation, I explored the availability of exceptionally

high-quality original images and found a wealth of them at the Library of Congress. The criteria for the photos I selected were that they had to be of excellent photographic quality and contain a high degree of human interest. I then began the arduous task of colorization. By the completion of the project, about as much time had elapsed creating the book as the duration of the war itself! The end result presents these wonderful and historic photographs in a way they have never been seen before—in true, life-like color. A way, I believe, that modern readers will find easier to relate to, to appreciate, and to comprehend as real events, experienced by real people, in a real world only slightly different from our own. ❖

– John Guntzelman
March 2011
Napili, Maui, HI

1

FELLOW CITIZENS

> " Fellow citizens, we cannot escape history.
> We of this congress and this administration will be remembered
> in spite of ourselves. No personal significance or insignificance
> can spare one or another of us. The fiery trial through which we pass
> will light us down in honor or dishonor to the latest generation. "

Abraham Lincoln

The Civil War is one of the first armed conflicts from which we have actual photographs of important figures as well as average soldiers. Before this time, paintings and sketches were the only likenesses of key persons available for future generations, and most paintings depicted a heroic, idealized nature of warfare and warriors.

Of the approximately four million soldiers who fought in the Civil War, a great number of them had their photographs taken by one of the estimated five thousand photographers doing business at the time. Most of those portraits were made into cartes de visite, or CDVs as they were popularly called. About the size of a visiting card, a CDV consisted of a small photograph pasted to a thicker 2 ½- by 4-inch paper card that could be autographed, traded, or swapped and was easily mailed to family members and friends. "Cartomania," as it was called, became very popular during the Civil War because of the novelty and relatively low cost of copies. Commercial CDVs of actors and actresses, army and government officials, and other nineteenth-century celebrities and notables were also made in great numbers, similar to modern-day trading cards.

A carte de visite photo was made on a glass wet-plate negative using a camera with multiple lenses, yielding four CDV images on each glass plate. The negative allowed

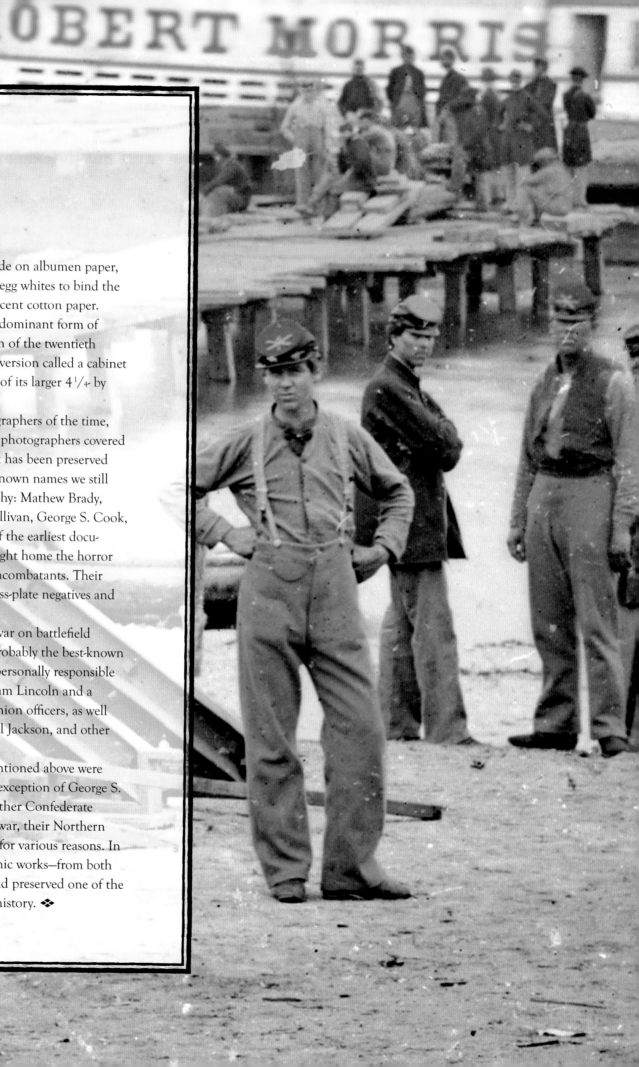

for any number of copies to be made on albumen paper, which used the albumen found in egg whites to bind the photographic chemicals to 100 percent cotton paper. These albumen prints became the dominant form of phtographic positives until the turn of the twentieth century. A slightly more expensive version called a cabinet card later became popular because of its larger 4 1/4 by 6 1/2-inch picture.

Beyond the common photographers of the time, a select group of nationally known photographers covered the war, and their remarkable work has been preserved it for us today. These are the well-known names we still associate with Civil War photography: Mathew Brady, Alexander Gardner, Timothy O'Sullivan, George S. Cook, and others. They produced some of the earliest documentary images of war, which brought home the horror and reality of combat for many noncombatants. Their photographs were also made on glass-plate negatives and reproduced on albumen paper.

In addition to shooting the war on battlefield locations, Mathew Brady—who is probably the best-known Civil War photographer—was also personally responsible for taking many portraits of Abraham Lincoln and a host of government officials and Union officers, as well as Robert E. Lee, General Stonewall Jackson, and other Confederates.

All of the photographers mentioned above were Northern photographers, with the exception of George S. Cook. Although there were many other Confederate photographers working during the war, their Northern counterparts became better known for various reasons. In any case, their collective photographic works—from both North and South—have captured and preserved one of the most turbulent times in American history. ❖

"**Abraham Lincoln,** sixteenth president of these United States, is everlasting in the memory of his countrymen." Thus he was described in Aaron Copland's 1942 orchestral work, *Lincoln Portrait.* As a young man, Lincoln held many positions, including part-owner of a general store in New Salem, Illinois; captain in the Illinois militia during the Black Hawk Indian War; postmaster of New Salem; and county surveyor. Lincoln only had about a year of formal education, but he was an insatiable reader who taught himself law.

He went on to become a lawyer, an Illinois state legislator, a member of the U.S. House of Representatives, and twice an unsuccessful candidate for the U.S. Senate. An outspoken opponent of slavery, Lincoln won the Republican nomination in 1860 and was subsequently elected president. His term in office was consumed with the American Civil War. Five days after Confederate forces surrendered on April 9, 1865, Lincoln became the first U.S. president to be assassinated. *(February 5, 1865. Alexander Gardner, photographer.)*

Jefferson Davis, president of the Confederate States of America. A graduate of West Point, Davis fought in the Mexican-American War as a colonel and was then appointed to the U.S. Senate in 1847 by the governor of Mississippi to complete the term of the late Senator Jesse Speight. When Franklin Pierce won the presidential election in 1852, he made Davis his secretary of war, charged with researching possible routes for the Transcontinental Railroad. Following his service in the Pierce administration, Davis was again elected as a U.S. senator from Mississippi. Although he argued against secession, he also fervently believed that each state had a sovereign right to secede if they so chose. Davis resigned from the U.S. Senate in January 1861, following Mississippi's secession. The next month he was provisionally appointed president of the Confederate States of America and elected to a six-year term that November. *(Date unknown. Mathew Brady, photographer.)*

Major General Ulysses S. Grant, officer of the Federal Army. Following his graduation from West Point in 1843, Grant successfully served as a lieutenant in the Mexican-American War. In 1861, he joined the Northern effort in the Civil War. Earning a reputation as one of the North's most aggressive generals, he rose quickly through the ranks. President Abraham Lincoln, impressed by Grant's willingness to fight and ability to win, appointed him lieutenant general in the regular army on March 2, 1864, and on March 12, Grant became general-in-chief of all the armies of the United States. By implementing a strategy of destroying the South's economy, as well as its military, Grant mounted a successful war of attrition against the Confederacy. He led the North to victory and accepted the surrender of General Robert E. Lee at Appomattox Court House, Virginia. He went on to become the eighteenth president of the United States. *(Date unknown. Mathew Brady, photographer.)*

Major General George G. Meade, officer of the Federal Army. Meade was a career U.S. Army officer and civil engineer who rose to the rank of commanding general of the Army of the Potomac. He defeated Confederate general Robert E. Lee and led the Union troops to victory at the Battle of Gettysburg in 1863. *(Date unknown. Mathew Brady, photographer.)*

General William T. Sherman, officer of the Federal army. The son of an Ohio Supreme Court justice, Sherman was acknowledged as an exceptional military commander and strategist. He received criticism for using a "scorched earth" strategy against the Confederacy—destroying and laying waste to anything potentially useful to the enemy. Sherman termed this strategy "hard war." While serving under General Grant, "Uncle Billy," as his troops called him, was instrumental in campaigns that led to the fall of Vicksburg and the defeat of the Confederates in Tennessee. Sherman succeeded General Grant as the Union commander in the western theater of the war in 1864. Following his capture of the city of Atlanta, he led his troops on the fabled "March to the Sea" through Georgia and the Carolinas, a campaign of "hard war" that was instrumental in demoralizing and destroying the Confederacy's ability to continue fighting. In April 1865, General Sherman accepted the surrender of Confederate armies of the Carolinas, Georgia, and Florida. *(Date unknown. Mathew Brady, photographer.)*

General Robert E. Lee, officer of the Confederate army. In early 1861, President Lincoln invited Lee to command the entire Union army. Lee declined because his home state of Virginia was seceding from the Union, despite Lee's personal wishes. In the newly established Confederacy, Lee served as a senior military adviser to President Jefferson Davis, until his first field command came in June of 1862, when he took control of the Confederate forces in the East, overseeing the Army of Northern Virginia. *(March 1864. Julian Vannerson, photographer.)*

General Thomas "Stonewall" Jackson, officer of the Confederate army. Considered by many military historians to be one of America's most gifted tactical commanders, Jackson is probably the most well-known Confederate commander after General Robert E. Lee. He prevailed at the battles of Bull Run (both first and second), Antietam, and Fredericksburg. His military glory was brought to an end on May 2, 1863, when Confederate pickets accidentally shot him after the Battle of Chancellorsville. The general survived the loss of an arm to amputation, but died of complications from pneumonia eight days later. His death was a severe blow for the Confederacy, affecting the morale of the army and of the general public alike. *(Date and photographer unknown.)*

"Damn the torpedoes, full speed ahead."

Rear Admiral David G. Farragut, officer of the Federal navy. He was the first full admiral of the U.S. Navy and is remembered for his alleged order at the Civil War Battle of Mobile Bay in Alabama: "Damn the torpedoes, full speed ahead!" *(Date unknown. Mathew Brady, photographer.)*

Major General Philip Sheridan, officer of the Federal army. A career U.S. Army officer, Sheridan rose quickly to the rank of major general. He was closely associated with Lieutenant General Ulysses S. Grant, who transferred Sheridan from command of an infantry division to lead the Cavalry Corps of the Army of the Potomac. In 1864, Sheridan defeated Confederate forces in the Shenandoah Valley, using what was looked upon as one of the first uses of "scorched earth" tactics in the war. In 1865, his cavalry doggedly pursued General Robert E. Lee and helped force his surrender at Appomattox. *(Date and photographer unknown.)*

Major General George Armstrong Custer, officer of the Federal army. During the Civil War, Custer acquired a solid reputation as an aggressive commander during the First Battle of Bull Run and the Appomattox Campaign, in which he and his troops played a decisive role. Custer was also on hand at General Robert E. Lee's surrender at Appomattox. After the war, Custer was sent west to fight in the Indian Wars, where he was defeated and killed at the Battle of the Little Bighorn, Montana Territory, in 1876. *(Date unknown. Mathew Brady, photographer.)*

Major General Benjamin F. Cheatham, officer of the Confederate army. At various times in his life, Cheatham was a Tennessee farmer, a California gold miner, and a Confederate general. He successfully served in many battles of the western theater, including the Battle of Shiloh and the Atlanta Campaign. (*Date and photographer unknown.*)

Major General George E. Pickett, officer of the Confederate army. Pickett was a career U.S. Army officer who resigned his commission and became a general in the Confederate army after his home state of Virginia seceded. He is best remembered for leading Pickett's Charge at the Battle of Gettysburg, which was a daring, ultimately futile attack by twelve thousand men who advanced over open fields for almost a mile under withering Union artillery and rifle fire. Although some Confederates were able to breach the low stone wall that shielded Union defenders, they could not hold their position and were repulsed with casualties of more than 50 percent. Their defeat ended three days of fighting at Gettysburg and concluded Lee's Pennsylvania Campaign. (*Date and photographer unknown.*)

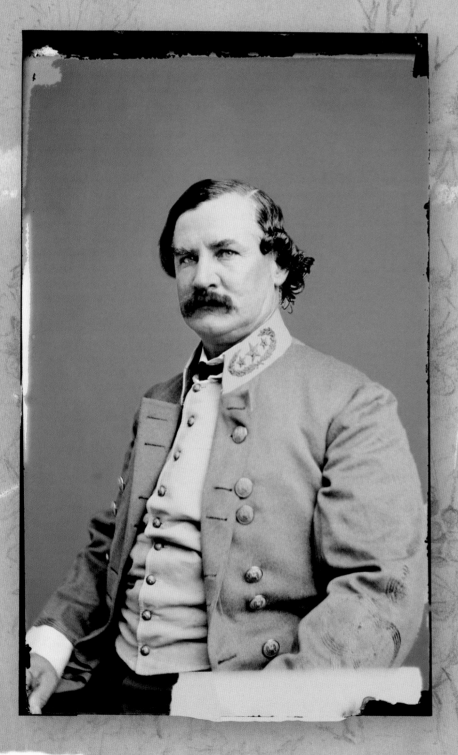

Brigadier General Joseph R. Anderson, officer of the Confederate army. In addition to being a Confederate general, Anderson was a civil engineer and an industrialist whose Tredegar Iron Works was a major weapons supplier for the Confederacy. *(Date and photographer unknown.)*

Brigadier General Richard L. T. Beale, officer of the Confederate army. Beale was commended for his intelligence and excellent judgment during many engagements. In December of 1862, he led an audacious expedition through the countryside near the Rappahannock River, capturing a Federal garrison without a single casualty. After the war, Beale resumed his political career. He was twice elected to Congress and, after retiring from public service, he resumed practicing law. *(Date and photographer unknown.)*

Major General Ambrose E. Burnside, officer of the Federal army. A native of Liberty, Indiana, Burnside graduated from the U.S. Military Academy at West Point in 1847. He was noted for his trademark facial hair, the style of which is now known as "sideburns"—a derivation of his last name. During his early military career he was wounded in the neck by an arrow while guarding U.S. mail routes from Apaches in New Mexico. When the Civil War began, Burnside was a brigadier general in the Rhode Island militia. While personally liked, he was looked upon as an incompetent commander. Although he led successful campaigns in North Carolina and Tennessee, he suffered disastrous defeats in the Battle of Fredericksburg and the Battle of the Crater. *(Date unknown. Mathew Brady, photographer.)*

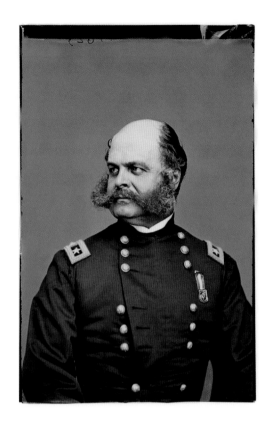

Major General Joseph Hooker, officer of the Federal army. Hooker was a career U.S. Army officer who had also fought in the Mexican-American War. He became a major general in the Union army and served with distinction throughout the war, although he is best known for his astonishing defeat by Robert E. Lee at the Battle of Chancellorsville in 1863. *(Date unknown. Mathew Brady, photographer.)*

"I had to go.
A spirit in
my feet
said 'Go,'
and I went."

B-1074

Mathew Brady, photographer. One of the most celebrated and well-known nineteenth-century American photographers, Brady's efforts to document the Civil War earned him a place in history. Despite the dangers and financial risks of bringing his photographic equipment onto battlefields, Brady later stated, "I had to go. A spirit in my feet said 'Go,' and I went." During the war, Brady spent more than $100,000 creating more than ten thousand glass-plate negatives, which he assumed the U.S. government would buy when the war ended. When the government refused, he had to sell his New York City studio and declare bankruptcy. *(Date and photographer unknown.)*

Unknown soldier from New York.
(Date and photographer unknown.)

Major John Roberts,
Confederate army. (Date and
photographer unknown.)

Unknown soldier from Ohio.
(Date and photographer unknown.)

Unknown soldier,
Confederate army. *(Date and photographer unknown.)*

CHICKAMAUGA BATTLEFIELD

SKETCHED BY
J. C. McELROY
OF THE
OHIO COMMISSION
Late Captain 18th Ohio Infantry.
1895.

FEDERAL LINES SEPT. 19. ▨▨▨▨ SEPT. 20.
CONFEDERATE LINES SEPT. 19. ▨▨▨▨ SEPT. 20.
OHIO MONUMENTS □ TABLETS ⬠

Private George Henry Graffam, age eighteen, Company B, 30th Maine Infantry. *(Date and photographer unknown.)*

Lieutenant Colonel James T. Weaver,
60th North Carolina Regiment.
(Date and photographer unknown.)

Corporal Nailer,
13th Pennsylvania Cavalry.
(Date and photographer unknown.)

Private Robert Patterson,
Company D, 12th Tennessee Infantry.
(Date and photographer unknown.)

Private Edwin Francis Jemison,
2nd Louisiana Regiment.
(Date and photographer unknown.)

Unknown horse artillery soldier, Federal army. *(Date and photographer unknown.)*

Private Walter Miles Parker, 1st Florida Cavalry. *(Date and photographer unknown.)*

Private George A. Stryker, New York Regiment.
(Date and photographer unknown.)

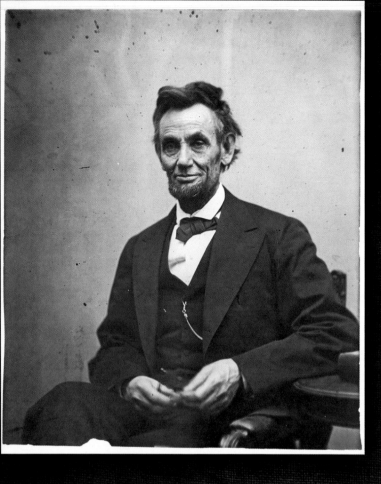

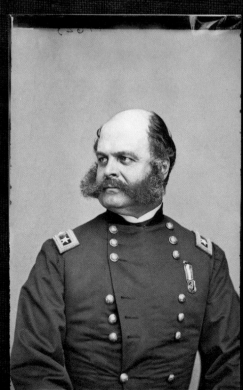

2

SLAVES, CONTRABANDS & FREEMEN

❝ As I would not be a slave, so I would not be a master.
This expresses my idea of democracy. Whatever differs from this,
to the extent of the difference, is no democracy. ❞

Abraham Lincoln

Slavery in the United States was one of the causes of the Civil War, but definitely not the only one. Other issues had to do with economic differences between the North and the South and, especially, states' rights versus federal rights.

According to the 1860 census, the overall population of the United States was approximately thirty-one million people when the Civil War began. Of that number, about twelve million people lived in the South, of which almost four million were in bondage as slaves.

Institutionalized slavery in North America actually originated in Virginia, the first English colony in the New World. In 1619, a Dutch ship arrived carrying a cargo of about twenty Africans, initiating a practice established in the New World Spanish colonies more than sixty years

earlier. The vast majority of slaves were black and were owned by whites, although some Native Americans and free blacks also had slaves. There was also a number of white indentured slaves. These people agreed to work for a period of time, usually four to seven years, in exchange for passage to the New World from Europe's overcrowded labor markets.

With Eli Whitney's 1793 invention of the cotton gin, which greatly reduced the time required to separate seeds from fibers, cotton became an extremely profitable crop. Consequently, many plantations moved from cultivating other cash crops to growing cotton for greater financial rewards. Cotton production expanded exponentially—especially in the South, where the climate and soil were favorable—requiring greater numbers of slaves to cultivate and harvest the crop. It was shown that farms with fifteen or more slaves proved to be far more productive than farms without slaves. Thus, the South became a one-crop economy, dependent on cotton—and therefore on slavery—to succeed. The Northern economy, by contrast, relied more on industry than agriculture, purchasing raw materials and turning them into finished goods. This key difference between the North and the South generated a major disparity in economic attitudes.

States' rights vs. federal rights were argued from the very inception of the United States. Following the American Revolution, the thirteen original states formed a confederation with a weak central government, as decreed by the Articles of Confederation, which was ratified in 1781. Problems with this form of government arose almost immediately. In 1787, the leaders of the time convened the Constitutional Convention, which resulted in the creation of the United States Constitution and established a stronger federal government. At the time of the Civil War, states' rights and the expansion of slavery to territories were especially contentious issues between the pro-slavery majority in the Southern states and the growing abolitionist, pro-Union movement in the North. When Abraham Lincoln was elected to the presidency in 1860, many Southern states were threatened by his anti-slavery stance and felt he was more in favor of Northern interests. As a result, seven states seceded from the Union before Lincoln was even inaugurated as president in March 1861.

Once the Southern states had seceded and the Civil War began, with the Battle of Fort Sumter on April 12, 1861, black slaves who fled behind Union lines were considered to be "contrabands." Prior to the war, escaped slaves would have been returned to their masters. Once the Southern states seceded from the Union, however, escaped slaves were deemed "contraband of war," since the Southern states were considered a foreign power by the United States. The first three slaves known to have escaped during the war had been instructed by their owner to assist the Confederate army in constructing defense batteries near the mouth of Hampton Roads, Virginia. They escaped at night by rowing a small boat across Hampton Roads Harbor, where they sought asylum at the Union-held Fort Monroe, commanded by General Benjamin Butler. The escaped slaves were kept as slaves by General Butler, who paid them nothing. Then, in late September of 1861, the secretary of the Union navy, Gideon Wells, issued an order that gave "persons of color, commonly known as contrabands," employment in the Union navy, with pay at the rate of ten dollars a month and a full day's ration. Three weeks later, the Union army began paying male contrabands eight dollars a month and females four dollars.

While becoming contraband did not mean full freedom, many slaves apparently saw it as a positive step in that direction; an estimated ten thousand slaves tried to gain contraband status in the North.

As members of the military, almost two hundred thousand African Americans fought for the Union in the Civil War. Approximately 10 percent of the Union army was black. Most were illiterate ex-slaves who had escaped to Union lines, though several thousand were well-educated free black men from Northern states. Following the Emancipation Proclamation of January 1, 1863, Abraham Lincoln said, "The colored population is the great available and yet unavailed of force for restoring the Union."

Many African American Civil War soldiers believed that military service allowed them to prove their right to equality, so they were eager to enlist in the Union army and join the fight against slavery. In fact, noted abolitionist Frederick Douglass firmly believed that allowing black men to fight would prove their right to citizenship and to vote. He said, "Once let the black man get upon his person the brass letters U.S., let him get an eagle on his button, and a musket on his shoulder and bullets in his pocket, there is no power on earth that can deny that he has earned the right to citizenship." By the end of the war, forty thousand black soldiers had died. Of the thirty-five hundred Federal soldiers buried at the Alexandria National Cemetery in Virginia, approximately two hundred and fifty are African Americans. ❖

Five generations of a black family on James Joyner "J. J." Smith's plantation in Beaufort, Port Royal Island, South Carolina. This family was photographed in 1862, after Union forces captured the Sea Island coastal area of South Carolina. These men and women were considered "contrabands of war" by the occupying Federal forces, which indicated that they had either escaped from bondage or had been liberated by Union soldiers. Famed Civil War photographer Timothy O'Sullivan visited this region from about November 1861 to March 1862. With the arrival of Union forces, Smith and other slaveholders fled, leaving behind large cotton plantations and thousands of slaves. *(1862. Timothy O'Sullivan, photographer.)*

A group of freed slaves, including men, women, and children, posing outside of a building at Foller's Plantation in Cumberland Landing, Pamunkey Run, Virginia. Using the term "contraband" to refer to escaped slaves emphasized their status as property. Such "contrabands" deprived the South of much-needed labor and also presented Union leaders with the problem of how to deal with them. *(May 14, 1862. James F. Gibson, photographer.)*

☛ A detail of the group at Foller's Plantation. By 1862, women and children contrabands would have been moved to confiscated Southern plantations, which were used to grow food for the Union army. The adult male contrabands were sent to assist the Army in more strenuous efforts, taking over support duties and work details, which freed up soldiers.

African Americans preparing cotton for the gin on the Smith plantation in Beaufort. This is another in the series of photographs taken by Timothy O'Sullivan during his visit to the area between late 1861 and early 1862. *(1862. Timothy O'Sullivan, photographer.)*

A closer view of African American contrabands preparing cotton for the gin. Note the earring worn by the woman in blue on the left.

"Contrabands." Two African American men sitting in front of an army tent in Culpeper, Virginia. (November 1863. Timothy O'Sullivan, photographer.)

An African American army cook at work near City Point, Virginia. In the early days of the war, freed slaves were not allowed to bear arms, so they often worked as cooks or were given other similar tasks.
(Date and photographer unknown.)

Company E of the 4th U.S. Colored Infantry Regiment
at Fort Lincoln, District of Columbia. The United States Colored
Troops (USCT), composed of African American soldiers, were
regiments of the U.S. Army during the Civil War. The men of the
USCT were the forerunners of the famous Buffalo Soldiers.
(Date unknown. William Morris Smith, photographer.)

☞ Following the Emancipation Proclamation on January 1, 1863,
African American men could legally be recruited into the Union army.
All-black units were formed, usually commanded by white officers.
These men are from Company E, 4th U.S. Colored Infantry, shown
in front of the Federal capital.

"Auction and Negro Sales." This photograph was taken while General William Tecumseh Sherman and his Union army occupied Atlanta, from September to November of 1864. The buildings shown are on Whitehall Street. *(1864. George Barnard, photographer.)*

African American soldiers in front of Major Strong's fortified quarters at Dutch Gap, Virginia. They are shown sitting outside a structure that was built into a hillside as protection from enemy artillery fire. *(November 1864. Photographer unknown.)*

African American teamsters
near the signal tower in Bermuda
Hundred, Virginia, a small town
near Richmond. In the colonial
era, the term "hundred" defined an
area large enough to support one
hundred households. The Bermuda
Hundred Campaign was a series
of battles fought in the town's
vicinity during May 1864.
(1864. Photographer unknown.)

A story in *Harper's Weekly*, March 7, 1863 stated, "In the Army of the Potomac there are probably from 8000 to 10,000 negroes employed as teamsters. This is a business they are well fitted for, and of course it relieves an equal number of white men for other duties. A teamster's life is a very hard one, particularly at this season of the year. It does not matter how much it storms, or how deep the mud, subsistence must be hauled to the camps, and day and night, toiling along with tired horses and mules, the creaking wagons are kept busy carrying to and fro commissary, quarter-master, and ordnance stores, in addition to keeping the camps supplied with fire-wood. White teamsters have $25 a month. Colored men are paid $20."

A group of African Americans by a canal in Richmond, Virginia. This group of "freedmen" posed along one of the canals in the heart of Richmond, with the ruins of Haxall's Mill in the background. Milling was one of the South's major industries, and flour made at this rolling mill, owned by Bolling Walker Haxall and his brothers, was shipped all over the world. The fire that ravaged the city following the Confederate withdrawal completely destroyed the facility. *(June 9, 1865. Alexander Gardner, photographer.)*

A picket station of African American troops at an abandoned farmhouse near the Dutch Gap Canal at Dutch Gap, Virginia. An advance guard post for a large military force was called a picket. Picket duty was the most hazardous work for infantrymen, because they would be the first to notice any major enemy movement and thus were the earliest to be killed, wounded, or captured. For that reason picket duty was rotated regularly within a regiment. *(November 1864. Photographer unknown.)*

"No advantage whatever was gained to compensate for the heavy loss we sustained."

African Americans collecting bones of soldiers killed in the Battle of Cold Harbor, Virginia. This battle was one of bloodiest, most uneven conflicts of the Civil War. Thousands of Union soldiers were killed or wounded in a futile frontal assault against Confederate troops. General Grant said of the battle, "I have always regretted that the last assault at Cold Harbor was ever made. . . . No advantage whatever was gained to compensate for the heavy loss we sustained." *(April 1865. John Reekie, photographer.)*

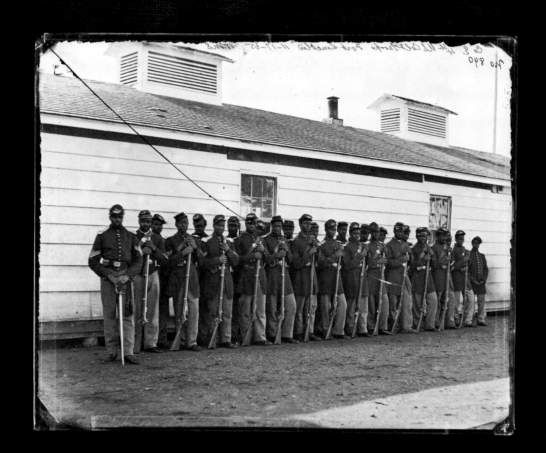

3

SOLDIERS
& CIVILIANS

" Four score and seven years ago our fathers brought forth,
upon this continent, a new nation, conceived in liberty, and dedicated
to the proposition that 'all men are created equal.'
Now we are engaged in a great civil war, testing whether that nation,
or any nation so conceived, and so dedicated, can long endure. "

Abraham Lincoln

The average age of the three million Union and Confederate Civil War soldiers was twenty-five when they enlisted; just slightly more than boys, they would soon be forged into men by the crucible of war. An estimated one hundred thousand Union soldiers were actually younger than fifteen, lying about their age to enlist because the minimum age was officially eighteen.

Prior to the war, soldiers on both sides worked a vast array of civilian jobs; the majority of them had been farmers. Very few of them had ever been away from home for any length of time. Once they became soldiers, they resided in the ubiquitous army camps of the Northern and the Southern armies.

Bustling cities made of canvas, partially obscured by smoke from hundreds of campfires, Civil War army camps were temporary, constantly changing residences used until the winter months when the armies would establish winter quarters. With the onset of cold weather, the soldiers would construct more permanent log huts large enough to accommodate several men. Soldiers often named their winter huts after well-known hotels and restaurants back home. The armies resided in these small huts throughout the winter and then moved back to the camps and canvas tents with the arrival of spring.

When not in battle, soldiers spent their free time in camp playing card games, writing letters home, reading, and playing sports such as baseball, which became very popular among Union soldiers during the war. Some soldiers even kept pets with them in camp—dogs, cats, squirrels, raccoons, and other creatures—in spite of regulations prohibiting it.

Very few Civil War soldiers had much formal education, although nearly 85 percent of them could read and write. Being separated from their families caused an unprecedented number of letters to be written between soldiers and their loved ones back home. The arrival of mail in camp was a cause for celebration since letters from home were a soldier's only connection with and reminder of the life he had left behind.

Sickness and disease in camp plagued both armies. It is estimated that for every man killed in battle, two died from disease because sanitation in the camps was so poor and medicine was very primitive. Whiskey was universally given for most ailments and as a painkiller, as was brandy and other spirits. Extremely ill soldiers were removed from camp and sent to brigade hospitals where their conditions usually worsened due to unsanitary conditions in the hospitals.

The United States Sanitary Commission was an official agency of the government created by legislation signed by President Lincoln on June 18, 1861. Its goal was to improve sanitation and to coordinate the volunteer efforts of women, many of whom wanted to contribute to the war effort. The volunteers raised money, worked as nurses in field hospitals, ran camp kitchens, administered hospital ships and soldiers' homes, made uniforms, and organized Sanitary Fairs to support the Federal army with funds and supplies. Southern women also sent medical supplies to help Confederate troops and provided nursing efforts in the camps, but there was no similar organization in the South comparable in scope to the USSC.

Collaborating with the Sanitary Commission to provide medical services, the United States Christian Commission was also an important organization during the Civil War. Five thousand USCC volunteers distributed more than six million dollars worth of goods and supplies (in 1860s valuation) to members of the Union army and navy. The organization also provided numerous social services and forms of recreation, in addition to their main goal of providing religious support to Union soldiers and sailors.

Religion played an important part in a soldier's daily routine. Many of the men attended army camp church services on a regular basis and some carried small Bibles with the rest of their baggage and equipment. Union and Confederate armies had numerous regimental and brigade chaplains. These officers also acted as assistants in field hospitals, comforting the sick and wounded and writing letters home for those who could not write. Chaplains held field services for their respective units, and many accompanied the soldiers as they marched onto the battlefield.

The food supplied to soldiers of both sides was plain and monotonous. Because the rations had to be transported long distances, commissary departments relied on foods that could be preserved for a long period of time, so the primary ingredients offered to Civil War soldiers were salted pork or beef and canned goods. Occasionally meat rations were boiled, broiled, or fried over open campfires. In place of bread, the Union army distributed a flour biscuit called hardtack, which soldiers nicknamed "tooth dullers," "worm castles," and "sheet iron crackers." During battles and when food was scarce, a Union soldier's primary source of food was often hardtack. Other food items included rice, peas, beans, dried fruit, potatoes, molasses, vinegar, and salt. Confederate soldiers were lucky if they received an adequate supply of cornmeal. The average Confederate soldier subsisted on bacon, cornmeal, ☞

molasses, peas, tobacco, vegetables, and rice. Coffee was considered a very desirable staple, and many soldiers—Northern and Southern—considered the ration of coffee, with its accompanying sugar, more important than anything else.

Early in the war, uniforms were provided by state militias, towns, and wealthy individuals, which initially resulted in a confusing variety of styles and colors on both sides. Over time, however, blue became the official color for the Northern Federalists and gray for the Southern Confederates. The most exotic and colorful uniforms were worn by militia units and volunteer drill teams called Zouaves. Their uniforms were patterned after and inspired by the Algerian Zouave units

of North Africa, known for their reputation as hard and fierce fighters. During the war, more than seventy volunteer Zouave units fought for the Union and twenty-five for the Confederacy.

The disruption and disorder caused by the Civil War was felt by virtually every citizen in all aspects of their lives, soldier and civilian alike. The various organizations mentioned in this section allowed women into areas of work and service they had never before experienced, just as young farmers were thrust into military situations most had never imagined. The remarkable photos that follow show the faces of Americans as they came face-to-face with war. ❖

Atop a makeshift flagpole, the Stars and Bars of the Confederacy flies over Fort Sumter in Charleston Harbor, South Carolina, following the thirty-four-hour bombardment that began the Civil War on April 12, 1861. *(Date and photographer unknown.)*

Tent life of the 31st Pennsylvania Infantry near Fort Slocum, one of the installations defending Washington, D.C. Early in the war, families occasionally followed their soldiers to army camps or periodically visited. The soldier holding the saw was probably the woman's husband and children's father. Note that for the occasion of the photograph, the family has displayed virtually all of their possessions in front of the tent. *(c. 1862. Photographer unknown.)*

Lieutenant George Armstrong Custer with a dog during the Peninsula Campaign in Virginia. Despite orders to the contrary, many soldiers kept animals as pets, and some units even had mascots. Custer seems to have been a dog lover and was photographed with them a number of times. *(1862. Photographer unknown.)*

General Isaac Ingalls Stevens (seated) and his staff on the porch of a house in Beaufort, South Carolina. Isaac I. Stevens was the first governor of Washington Territory, a U.S. congressman, and a major general in the Union army. General Stevens occupied Beaufort less than a year after South Carolina seceded, making it one of the first communities in the Deep South to be held in Union hands. This photo was taken about six months before Stevens died in action at the Battle of Chantilly after picking up the fallen flag of his old regiment. Struck in the temple by a bullet, he died instantly on September 1, 1862. *(March 1862. Timothy O'Sullivan, photographer.)*

Federal cavalry at Sudley Ford following the First Battle of Bull Run in July 1861. That clash, also known as the Battle of Manassas, was the first major land battle of the Civil War and a stunning Confederate victory. The Southern army held their position in Virginia, causing great concern in the North of a possible invasion of Washington, D.C. In early March 1862, however, Confederate forces withdrew and assumed new positions south of the Rappahannock River in eastern Virginia. Union troops under General George McClellan then began advancing up the Virginia Peninsula to Richmond. Union cavalry are seen here crossing Sudley Ford. *(March 1862. George Barnard, photographer.)*

☛ A closer view of local children observing Union cavalry soldiers across Sudley Ford. The two girls, probably sisters, wear dresses made from the same fabric. Also notice the torn pants on the taller boy.

A **Union Army supply base** at Cumberland Landing on the Pamunkey River in eastern Virginia. This sizeable camp, essentially a city of tents, was part of Union general George McClellan's Peninsula Campaign, which was an attempt to take Richmond with an army of 100,000 men. The maneuver, probably the single largest Union operation of the war, failed. In spite of reaching within a few miles of Richmond, McClellan never made a direct assault on the Confederate capital. *(May 1862. James F. Gibson, photographer.)*

The Lines at Yorktown. Virginia April 30th 1862

Armaments and supplies ready for transport from the Federal artillery park at Yorktown, Virginia, to White House Landing on the Pamunkey River. White House Landing was a major Union supply base during General George McClellan's Peninsula Campaign in 1862. Its name derived from the adjacent White House Plantation owned by the family of Martha Custis, the widow who married George Washington. *(May 1862. Photographer unknown.)*

☛ A closer view of Federal soldiers at the Yorktown supply depot. Note that they have been made aware of the photographer and most have turned toward the camera to pose for the photograph.

The staff of General Fitz-John Porter, with Lieutenant George Armstrong Custer reclining on the right, somewhere on the Virginia Peninsula. Porter was a career U.S. Army officer and a Union general during the Civil War. Although Porter served well in early battles, he was found guilty of disobeying a lawful order and removed from command by political rivals. The court-martial was later overturned, and Porter was reinstated in the U.S. Army. *(May 20, 1862. James F. Gibson, photographer.)*

Captain James Madison Robertson (third from left) and his officers at Fair Oaks, Virginia. Captain Robertson commanded the combined Battery B and Battery L of the 2nd U.S. Artillery during the Peninsula Campaign in 1862. He was then chosen as the commander of the U.S. Horse Artillery Brigade and held that position until the end of the war. Robertson fought in most of the major battles in the eastern theater. (June 1862. James F. Gibson, photographer.)

2358

The Federal artillery park at Yorktown, Virginia.

The Battle of Yorktown was fought from April 5 to May 4, 1862. In mid-March, hundreds of ships transported an army of more than 120,000 men led by Union general George McClellan to Fort Monroe on the tip of the Virginia Peninsula. From there McClellan planned to attack the Confederate capital of Richmond and bring the war to a quick conclusion. Marching from Fort Monroe on April 5, his army encountered General John Magruder's small Confederate army at Yorktown. McClellan suspended the march up the peninsula, ordered the construction of siege fortifications, and brought his heavy siege guns to the front. In the meantime, Confederate general Joseph Johnston brought reinforcements for Magruder. McClellan's siege preparations were huge, consisting of fifteen batteries with more than seventy heavy guns, including two 200-pound and twelve 100-pound Parrott rifles. The rest of the weaponry included 20- and 30-pounders, 4.5-inch Rodman siege rifles, and forty-one mortars ranging in size from 8 to 13 inches. If fired in unison, these batteries could have delivered more than 7,000 pounds of shells onto the enemy positions with each volley. For the remainder of April, the Confederates improved their defenses while McClellan's men moved the massive artillery batteries. Johnston knew that the impending bombardment would be difficult to withstand, so he began sending his supply wagons in the direction of Richmond. Escaped slaves reported that fact to McClellan, but he refused to believe them. He was convinced that an army whose size he estimated at almost 120,000 men would stay and fight. On the evening of May 3, the Confederates launched a brief bombardment of their own and then fell silent. Early next morning, the Union army found that the Confederates had slipped away, leaving their earthworks empty. *(Date and photographer unknown.)*

☞ A closer view of Union troops and massive stores of armament and weaponry at the artillery park in Yorktown, Virginia.

The Grapevine Bridge, built by the 5th New Hampshire
Infantry, at the Chickahominy River in Virginia. The bridge,
named by General Edwin Sumner after its twisted and winding
structure, was completed on the night of May 29, 1862. Heavy
rains the next night loosened the supports so much that
when General Sumner led his troops across the overpass, only
the weight of the marching column kept the logs in place.
Sumner's initiative in sending reinforcement troops across the
dangerously rain-swollen river prevented the Battle of Seven
Pines at Fair Oaks, Virginia, from becoming a Union disaster.
(June 1862. D. B. Woodbury, photographer.)

☛ A closer view of members of the 5th New Hampshire
Infantry at work strengthening the upper bridge across the
Chickahominy River. Commanded by Colonel Edward Cross,
members of this unit were able to construct the Grapevine
Bridge over a period of only two days.

Standing by a three-inch ordnance rifle at Fair Oaks, Virginia, are, from left to right, Lieutenant Robert Clarke, Captain John C. Tidball, Lieutenant William N. Dennison, and Captain Alexander C. M. Pennington. Under the command of Captain Tidball, Battery A was among the most prominent units in the U.S. Horse Artillery Brigade. It was equipped with three sections, each with a pair of three-inch ordnance rifles. (*June 1862. James Gibson, photographer.*)

Confederate fortifications reinforced with bales of cotton during the Battle of Yorktown, Virginia. Fought from April 5 to May 4, 1862, this battle occurred near the site of the final battle of the American Revolution, of the same name. At Yorktown, General George McClellan's Union army encountered a small Confederate force, whose purposefully noisy troop and weaponry movements suggested a much larger Confederate presence.

The Union army settled into a siege posture and commenced an artillery duel. This photo was made after Confederate troops abandoned Yorktown, which was then taken over by the Northern army. Note the soldier in the foreground sitting atop the base of a destroyed canon and the ruptured bales of cotton, which were used in addition to sandbags. *(June 1862. Photographer unknown.)*

A Federal battery near Fair Oaks, Virginia. The Battle of Fair Oaks, or Fair Oaks Station, was the culmination of Union general George McClellan's Peninsula Campaign, in which his army reached the very outskirts of Richmond, but could go no farther. Although inconclusive, it was the largest battle in the eastern theater up to that time, with more than five thousand Union and six thousand Confederate casualties. After the battle, McClellan wrote, "I am tired of the sickening sight of the battlefield, with its mangled corpses and poor suffering wounded! Victory has no charms for me when purchased at such cost." *(June 1862. Photographer unknown.)*

Union general Ambrose E. Burnside (reading newspaper) with photographer Mathew Brady (in front of tree) and others at the Army of the Potomac headquarters in Cold Harbor, Virginia. *(June 1864. Photographer unknown.)*

☞ A closer view of General Ambrose E. Burnside and Mathew Brady. The general's distinctive facial hair gave rise to the term "sideburns." Brady is probably the best-known Civil War photographer. He employed Alexander Gardner, Timothy O'Sullivan, and George Barnard, as well as almost twenty others. Brady was in the field every year of the war, taking photographs, as well as directing and organizing his associates.

A Union field hospital after the Battle of Savage's Station in Virginia. Fought on June 27, this was the fourth of the "Seven Days Battles," a series of six major battles over seven days from June 25 to July 1, 1862. Confederate general Robert E. Lee drove General George McClellan's Union army away from Richmond and into retreat down the Virginia Peninsula. *(June 30, 1862. James Gibson, photographer.)*

The battlefield at Cedar Mountain, Virginia, viewed from the west. The Battle of Cedar Mountain took place on August 9, 1862. After nearly being driven from the field early in battle, Confederate troops led by General Stonewall Jackson counterattacked and broke the Union lines, resulting in a Confederate victory. *(August 1862. Timothy O'Sullivan, photographer.)*

Blacksmiths shoeing horses at the headquarters of the Army of the Potomac at Antietam, Maryland. The United States is estimated to have had about 7.5 million horses at the beginning of the Civil War. The number used in the war is not known, although horses were the backbone of both the North and South armies: moving guns, ambulances, and ammunition, carrying messages, and being ridden in cavalry units. *(September 1862. Alexander Gardner, photographer.)*

☛ A closer view of a field blacksmith operation. All of the Union and Confederate animals needed farrier services, so blacksmiths brought forges to the battlefields for shoeing horses, as well as for repairing damaged metal items.

Men repairing a single-track railroad after the Battle of Stones River near Murfreesboro, Tennessee. This battle was fought from December 31, 1862 to January 2, 1863, and was the culmination of the Union army's Stones River Campaign. Stones River had the highest percentage of casualties on both sides out of all the major battles of the Civil War. Although the battle itself was inconclusive, the Confederate withdrawal gave a boost to Union morale after their earlier defeat at Fredericksburg. (1863. Photographer unknown.)

Clerks of the Commissary Depot at Aquia Creek Landing, Virginia. Aquia Creek is a tributary of the Potomac River in Northern Virginia, and the landing there was alternately occupied by both armies throughout 1861 and 1862, until the Union was finally able to establish and defend a supply depot there. The primary job of the commissary department was to locate, distribute, and supply food to the various armies in the field. In this obviously staged photo, the clerks appear as quite dapper individuals being served coffee by an African American contraband. *(February 1863. Alexander Gardner, photographer.)*

General Robert E. Lee's headquarters on the Chambersburg Pike at Gettysburg, Pennsylvania. At the time of the Civil War, the house was owned by noted statesman Thaddeus Stevens, but was the dwelling place of Mrs. Mary Thompson, known to the residents of Gettysburg as "Widow" Thompson. On July 1, 1863, Lee established his personal headquarters in the old house, which was chosen by his staff, not only because of its close proximity to the battlefield, but also because the thick stone walls afforded the general some physical protection from artillery shells. *(July 1863. Photographer unknown.)*

No 346

HEADQUARTERS
POST OFFICE.

2127

A group in front of a post office tent for the Army of the
Potomac at Falmouth, Virginia. This post office was established at the
headquarters of the Army of the Potomac, with William B. Haslett
serving as the Army postmaster. Every day the post office distributed
thousands of letters to Union soldiers in the field. The sending
and delivery of mail was an immensely important factor for troop
morale—it was a soldier's only connection to the lives and loves he
had left behind. *(April 1863. Timothy O'Sullivan, photographer.)*

Alfred Rudolph Waud, artist for *Harper's Weekly*, sketching on the battlefield at Gettysburg, Pennsylvania. Waud was a London-born American illustrator who joined *Harper's Weekly* as a full-time staff artist in 1861. During the war, all images for publication had to be drawn by hand because there was no way of transferring a photograph to a printing plate. An artist such as Waud would make detailed sketches in the field, which were then rushed by courier back to the main office. The drawings were then engraved onto a block of wood for integration into the printing process. *(July 1863. Timothy O'Sullivan, photographer.)*

John L. Burns, the "Old Hero of Gettysburg." An actual news article from the *Gettysburg Gazette* of July 10, 1863: "Seventy-two year old John L. Burns dropped everything to fight for his country in the Battle of Gettysburg. From his house, Burns could see the armies of the Union and Confederacy locked in battle at Gettysburg. At first he stopped what he was doing and just watched. Then he grabbed his rifle and ran to fight when the 150th Pennsylvania came to reinforce the Union forces at the end of the first day. Burns fought successfully on the second day, but he was wounded on the third, probably as he was defending the ridge against Pickett's charge. Even though wounded, he kept fighting until the battle was over. Since he was not a regular solider, he simply went home at the battle's end and resumed his normal life." *(July 1863. Timothy O'Sullivan, photographer.)*

Noncommissioned officers of Company D, 93rd New York Infantry, eating dinner near Bealeton, Virginia. *(August 1863. Timothy O'Sullivan, photographer.)*

Field headquarters of the United States Christian Commission in Germantown, Virginia. Formed in the fall of 1861 by the Young Men's Christian Association (YMCA), the USCC was a Christian-based organization for civilian men and women wishing to help the war effort. Following the disastrous First Battle of Bull Run, the YMCA's National Committee convened in New York City to determine what could be done to support the soldiers. The charter of the USCC was established the next day. Members of the USCC were called "delegates." Some volunteers were seminary students, but most were just concerned Christians with a desire to help soldiers. During the war, there were approximately five thousand USCC delegates who distributed goods and supplies on battlefields and in camps, hospitals, and prisons. *(August 1863. Photographer unknown.)*

A group at the tent and wagon of the *New York Herald* in Bealeton, Virginia. The Civil War created a tremendous demand for news. For the first time, reporters actually traveled to the frontlines, establishing a new breed of journalist: the war correspondent. Reporters would telegraph dispatches back to their newspapers on a daily basis so that news and information could be printed the following day. In 1861, the *New York Herald* had a distribution of eighty-four thousand and called itself "the most largely circulated journal in the world." Owner James Gordon Bennett strongly supported the Union, but the paper was a constant source of condemnation of Lincoln and his policies. New York's Herald Square is named after the newspaper, which housed its headquarters in the area. *(August 1863. Timothy O'Sullivan, photographer.)*

Drum Corps of the 93rd New York Infantry at Bealeton, Virginia. Drums performed an important function in battlefield communications. In addition to setting a cadence for marching, various drum rolls communicated different commands and signals. During combat, a drummer boy would usually stand near an officer so that he could instantly alert the troops with appropriate drum rolls. Boys were usually recruited for the job so as to free up men for combat duty. The life of a Civil War drummer boy appeared to be glamorous, so boys of all ages often ran away from home to enlist. Officially there were age restrictions, but those were often ignored, and boys as young as ten or twelve were occasionally given the job. *(August 1863. Timothy O'Sullivan, photographer.)*

Provost Marshal and General Marsena R. Patrick and his staff at Culpeper, Virginia. Provost marshals are the officers in charge of military police. After the Battle of Antietam and the subsequent reorganization of the command structure, Patrick was named provost marshal for the Army of the Potomac on October 6, 1862. To support his office, he had the equivalent of a brigade of troops at his command. When General "Fighting Joe" Hooker became the new commander of the Army of the Potomac on January 26, 1863, he had Patrick form the Bureau of Military Information, a network of intelligence agents. At the Battle of Gettysburg, Patrick was responsible for processing thousands of Confederate prisoners of war. In early 1864, when Ulysses S. Grant was placed in command of all Union armies, Patrick was elevated to provost marshal for the combined forces operating against Richmond, Virginia. *(September 1863. Timothy O'Sullivan, photographer.)*

A newspaper vendor at his cart selling papers in camp. The nation was starved for current news during the Civil War, and newspapers were the most reliable and expedient source of news. They not only took news of the war back to the rest of the country, but also brought news from home to the soldiers. *(November 1863. Alexander Gardner, photographer.)*

A **Union encampment** on the edge of Culpeper, Virginia. Both Union and Confederate forces occupied the town, which was the site of a number of important Civil War battles at different times during the war. More than 17,000 saber-wielding horsemen and 3,000 infantry troops clashed at nearby Brandy Station on June 9, 1863, making it the largest cavalry battle of the War. The Union army's winter encampment of that year, which numbered almost 120,000 soldiers, was the largest encampment of the Civil War. *(November 1863. Timothy O'Sullivan, photographer.)*

Wilson's Command
Portion of Gen' Wilson's Cav. dismounted
(1) Gen Wood's position
(3)   Do   attack 4.4 P.M. Dec. 15.
(2)   Do   carries position at 1.0'c P.M.

Part of Wilson's Cavalry attacking
"   "   pursuing enemy
Smith & Schofield attacking

Rebel Works   Union Works

SOLDIERS & CIVILIANS   105

The railroad yard and depot at Nashville, Tennessee, with the state capitol building in the distance. Beginning in late February 1862, Union troops moved into Nashville and occupied it for the remainder of the Civil War. In December 1864, Confederate general John Bell Hood's Army of the Tennessee tried to recapture Nashville. Union forces led by General George H. Thomas countered his attack. The resulting two-day battle crushed Hood's army, leaving Nashville securely under Union control. (*1864. George Barnard, photographer.*)

A closer view of the Nashville railroad depot, with passengers milling about. George Barnard took this photograph, along with others taken around the city, during his time as an official Union army photographer in Nashville in 1864. Notice the beautifully detailed paint job and brass fittings on the locomotives, which were typical of railroad engines of that time.

BATTLEFIELDS IN FRONT OF NASHVILLE

where the United States Forces commanded by

Union soldiers relaxing by the guns of a captured Confederate fort near Atlanta, Georgia. After months of relentless fighting around the area, Sherman forced Confederate general John Bell Hood to abandon Atlanta, the munitions center of the Confederacy. Sherman remained there, resting his men and accumulating supplies, for nearly two and a half months. (*1864. George Barnard, photographer.*)

Union general William Tecumseh Sherman on horseback, opposite, at Federal Fort No. 7 near Atlanta. On September 1, 1864, Confederate forces evacuated Atlanta after a four-month siege by Sherman's army. The following day, Atlanta mayor James Calhoun surrendered the city to Sherman, who sent a telegram to President Lincoln reading, "Atlanta is ours, and fairly won." This victorious capture of Atlanta helped to ensure Lincoln's reelection in November 1864. Before Atlanta, it had appeared likely that the Democratic Party's candidate, General George B. McClellan, would defeat Lincoln. Following the November elections, Sherman's army of 62,000 men began a march to the port city of Savannah, Georgia—Sherman's famous "March to the Sea." To break the South's will to continue fighting, Sherman used a tactic he called "hard war," whereby his army lived off of the land and destroyed almost everything in its path. On December 21, 1864, his troops captured Savannah, which he referred to as a Christmas present for President Lincoln. (*1864. George Barnard, photographer.*)

A field telegraph station at Wilcox's Landing, near Charles City Court House, Virginia. When the war began, telegraph became the most important form of military communication, so mobile telegraph units were developed that could travel along with the forces. By the end of the war, more than fifteen thousand miles of telegraph lines had been built. Along with the telegraph, many other technological advances occurred as a direct result of Civil War needs. This photograph was made during General Grant's Wilderness Campaign of May and June 1864. *(1864. Photographer unknown.)*

A Civil War photographer and his portable darkroom wagon at a signal tower in Bermuda Hundred, Virginia. The North and the South used a system of signal towers for sending messages in areas where telegraph wires had not yet been strung. Towers like this one relayed critical messages and troop movement instructions via codes transmitted by the use of semaphore flags. *(1864. Photographer unknown.)*

Adams Express office for the Army of the James at Bermuda Hundred, Virginia. The Adams Express Company, a competitor of Wells, Fargo and Company, was incorporated in 1854 and was the paymaster for the Union army during the Civil War. (*1864. Photographer unknown.*)

☞ A closer view of military and civilian personnel at an Adams Express office. Interestingly, the company also served as paymaster for the Confederate army through its subsidiary, Southern Express, a Georgia corporation formed in 1861. Note the soldier second from right wearing a Zouave uniform.

Officers and ladies on the porch of a garrison house at Fort Monroe, Virginia. Located in Hampton Roads, Virginia, on the peninsula overlooking Chesapeake Bay, Fort Monroe was the only Federal military installation in the upper South to remain under United States control throughout the entire Civil War. President Lincoln's blockade of Southern port cities was centered around the fort. In cooperation with the Federal navy, troops from Fort Monroe extended Union control along the Confederate coastline all the way to the Gulf of Mexico. (*1864. Photographer unknown.*)

Three officers of the 1st Connecticut Heavy Artillery posing for a photograph at Fort Brady, Virginia. Fort Brady was an earthen structure, rather than one made of bricks like many forts. Union gunners and artillerymen stationed there found their tour of duty unsettling and occasionally dangerous. From October 1864 through April 1865, Union troops occupying the fort were frequently shelled by Confederate artillery batteries across the James River, and one major assault in early 1865 caused numerous Union casualties. *(1864. Photographer unknown.)*

Union soldiers pose at the entrance of an ammunition magazine at Fort Brady, Virginia. "Magazines" for storage of ammunition, from bullets to cannon shells, were normally covered with earth for protection from incoming shells and to lessen the danger of explosion. *(1864. Photographer unknown.)*

The railroad depot at Atlanta, Georgia. Although it was just a relatively small town of about ten thousand people before the war, Atlanta was a vital transportation center, connected by major roads and rail systems with other cities throughout the South. During the war, the population doubled as the city became the center for Confederate quartermasters who warehoused and shipped food, clothing, ammunition, and other supplies needed by Confederate armies. This photograph was taken after General Sherman occupied Atlanta on September 2, 1864. When his army departed the city two months later, the railway depot, as well as much of the city, was destroyed. As Sherman recounted in his memoirs, "Behind us lay Atlanta, smoldering and in ruins, the black smoke rising high in the air, and hanging like a pall over the ruined city." *(1864. George Barnard, photographer.)*

Nurses and officers of the United States Sanitary Commission at Fredericksburg, Virginia. The USSC was an official agency of the United States government, whose purpose was to promote clean and healthy conditions in Union army camps. The Commission raised money, provided supplies, staffed field hospitals, and worked to educate the military on matters of health and sanitation. Many women volunteered to work with the Sanitary Commission, some working as field hospital nurses or performing other medical tasks, while others raised money and managed the organization. *(May 20, 1864. James Gardner, photographer.)*

☛ A closer view of USSC nurses and officers. Based on their Sanitary Commission experience, many of the volunteers found work after the Civil War in jobs that had previously been closed to women. Others, unable to find such opportunities in the work force, became activists for women's rights, while many simply returned home to traditional female roles as wives and mothers.

A "council of war" held at the Massaponax Church in Fredericksburg, Virginia. The church's location placed it directly in the midst of activity on many occasions during the Civil War. Here, Union commanders, including General Ulysses S. Grant, General George G. Meade, Assistant Secretary of War Charles A. Dana, and numerous staff officers, have removed pews from inside the church in order to hold a council of war in front of the building. *(May 21, 1864. Timothy O'Sullivan, photographer.)*

☛ A much closer view of the famous photograph of the Massaponax Church council of war. The man in brown moved his head during the interval of exposure and so is blurred. Seated next to him is an unmistakable and remarkably candid view of General Grant with his ever-present cigar. On the left of the image, General Meade, in the slouched hat, is looking over some paperwork or a map.

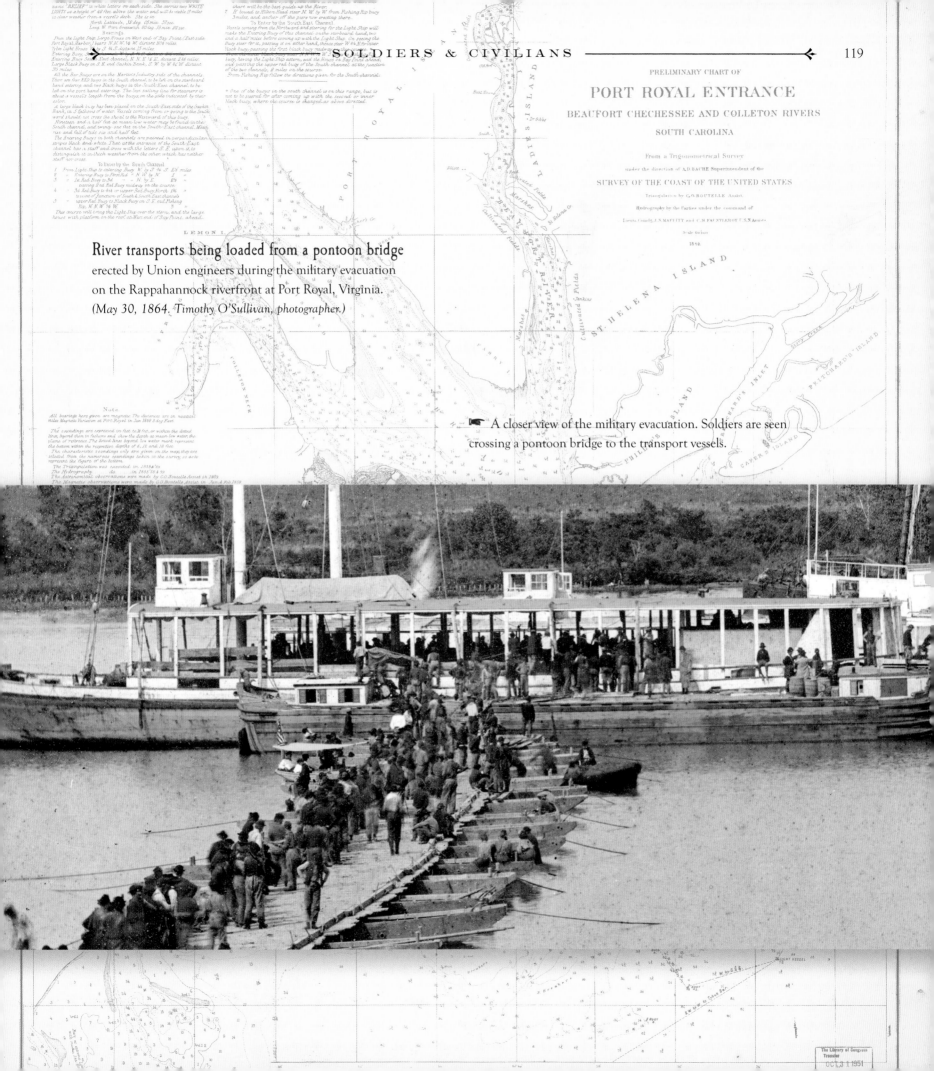

River transports being loaded from a pontoon bridge erected by Union engineers during the military evacuation on the Rappahannock riverfront at Port Royal, Virginia. (*May 30, 1864. Timothy O'Sullivan, photographer.*)

A closer view of the military evacuation. Soldiers are seen crossing a pontoon bridge to the transport vessels.

General Ulysses S. Grant at his headquarters in Cold Harbor, Virginia, left. At Cold Harbor, Grant's army was stopped by Lee's Army of Northern Virginia as Grant tried to move around Lee's right flank. After two days of skirmishes, Grant mounted a flawed frontal assault on the Confederate positions. In just half an hour, seven thousand Union soldiers were killed or wounded, while the Confederates lost fewer than fifteen hundred men. *(June 1864. Edgar Guy Fowx, photographer.)*

A group from Company D, U.S. Engineer Battalion, at Petersburg, Virginia. During the Civil War, engineering units were responsible for building pontoon and railroad bridges, constructing forts and batteries, and creating roadways. They also orchestrated the destruction of enemy supply lines. The engineer corps was essential in making the war effort logistically feasible. *(August 1864. Photographer unknown.)*

Overleaf: A group of Company G Zouaves of the 114th Pennsylvania Infantry at Petersburg, Virginia. At the beginning of the Civil War, state militia units became the basis for many of the Zouave units that fought during the war. This particular regiment was formed in the city of Philadelphia on August 17, 1861. Known then as the Zouaves d'Afrique, the company was integrated into the U.S. Army early in the Civil War. Throughout the war, they served in numerous battles with courage and distinction. Prior to the Battle of Petersburg, the regiment was frequently sent into the trenches and employed in difficult picket duty. In the final attack on the defenses of Petersburg, the regiment was put on the front line and stormed "Fort Hell," so called after repeated failures by other troops. On the following morning, they had the satisfaction of unfurling the U.S. flag over the courthouse of Petersburg. Zouave uniforms became immensely popular and influenced everything from state militia uniforms to women's clothing. *(August 1864. Photographer unknown.)*

Officers of the 114th Pennsylvania Infantry
playing cards in front of their tents at Petersburg,
Virginia. Men of the 114th Pennsylvania saw
active service from the fall of 1862 until the spring
of 1865, in the campaigns of Fredericksburg,
Chancellorsville, Gettysburg, and Petersburg.
(August 1864. Photographer unknown.)

☛ A closer view of the obviously staged photograph
of Pennsylvania infantrymen playing cards. When
not in battle, most soldiers spent their time reading,
writing letters home, or playing card games to take
their minds off the war.

Mills on the Appomattox River near Campbell's
Bridge at Petersburg, Virginia. Located twenty-three miles
south of the Confederate capital of Richmond, Petersburg
was another of the South's primary transportation hubs.
The city was also a vital manufacturing center, boasting
iron foundries, tobacco firms, and flour and cotton mills.
As the seventh largest Confederate city, with a population
of nearly nineteen thousand residents, Petersburg citizens
were divided almost equally between blacks and whites.
(*May 1865. Timothy O'Sullivan, photographer.*)

The Petersburg, Virginia, courthouse. After nine
months of trench warfare, Confederate general Robert E. Lee
finally yielded to overwhelming Union pressure and abandoned
Petersburg. The fall of the city also signaled that the Confederate
capital of Richmond could no longer be defended, forcing Lee
into his last march of retreat. (*1865. Photographer unknown.*)

General Sherman's troops using wheelbarrows to remove ammunition from Fort McAllister near Savannah, Georgia. The Second Battle of Fort McAllister took place on December 13, 1864, near the end of Sherman's "March to the Sea." The Union army overwhelmed a small Confederate force defending the strategically important fort. Sherman was then able to prepare for the siege and capture of Savannah, a goal he would achieve by Christmas. *(December 1864. Photographer unknown.)*

Fire Engine No. 3, Richmond, Virginia. In the 1800s, fire was an incredible danger in municipalities. Because most buildings were constructed from wood, the war posed an especially grave danger of fire. A fire that began in a single building could quickly spread and destroy an entire section of a city or town. Local firefighters, in many cases volunteers, were the only defense against the total disaster that fire could cause. The pumper shown here was pulled by horses to the site of a fire, but the pumping mechanism was operated by hand. This type of pumper needed access to a ready source of water—a well, river, or stream—from which to pump the water. *(1865. Photographer unknown.)*

Interior of the Confederate's Fort Darling on the James River at Drewry's Bluff, Virginia. This fort was the site of the Battle of Drewry's Bluff on May 15, 1862, when five U.S. Navy gunboats, including the ironclads *Monitor* and *Galena*, steamed up the James River to test Richmond's defenses. They encountered submerged obstacles and deadly accurate fire from the batteries at Fort Darling, which inflicted severe damage on *Galena*. Consequently, the Federal navy was turned back. *(1865. Photographer unknown.)*

A mounted gun parapet at Fort Moultrie in Charleston, South Carolina. The forts surrounding Charleston Harbor—Moultrie, Sumter, Johnson, and Castle Pinckney—formed a circle of defense for the city. When South Carolina seceded from the Union in December of 1860, the Union garrison abandoned Fort Moultrie for the better fortified Fort Sumter. Four months later, Confederate shelling forced Sumter to surrender, and the Confederates occupied the forts. In April 1863, Union shore batteries and ironclads initiated a twenty-month bombardment of forts Sumter and Moultrie, yet Charleston's defenses held. When the Confederate army finally evacuated the city in February 1865, Fort Moultrie again came under Union occupation, which was when this photograph was taken. *(1865. Photographer unknown.)*

A Civil War sutler's shelter at Petersburg, Virginia. Sutlers were civilian merchants who followed the troops during the Civil War and sold them provisions. This particular facility has been named the "Fruit and Oyster House," most likely after an existing restaurant or store. There would be scant opportunity of getting either fruit or oysters on the battlefield. *(Date unknown. Timothy O'Sullivan, photographer.)*

Federal soldiers in front of a shellproof shelter at Fort Burnham, formerly a Confederate stronghold, Fort Harrison, in Virginia. On September 29, 1864, twenty-five Union forces overran and captured Fort Harrison, the most well-defended Confederate fort on the Richmond-Petersburg line. The fort was then renamed Fort Burnham in honor of General Hiram Burnham, who had been killed in the attack. *(Date and photographer unknown.)*

A view across the Chain Bridge over the Potomac River in Washington, D.C. This bridge, which connected Washington with Virginia, was an important and heavily defended crossing point of the Potomac River. An earlier bridge at that location was built of large chain-linked trusses. The new bridge of heavy wooden crossbeams framed by long arches was erected in 1852, although the original name stuck for its replacement. *(1865. William Morris Smith, photographer.)*

A group in front of the United States Christian Commission storehouse in Washington, D.C. Similar to the United States Sanitary Commission, the United States Christian Commission also provided nursing care with the objective of improving the moral condition of soldiers. The USCC passed out many religious books and Bibles and provided food, coffee, and even liquor to soldiers in army camps. The organization is estimated to have raised about 6.25 million dollars (1860 valuation) in money and supplies. *(April 1865. Photographer unknown.)*

☞ A closer view of members of the USCC at the Washington, D.C. storehouse. Note how everyone has dressed especially well for the occasion of having their photograph taken—an event in the 1860s. Also notice the various markings and addresses on the shipping cases.

Brigadier General Rufus Ingalls (seated, center, in uniform) and a group at City Point, Virginia. Ingalls was the chief quartermaster for the Army of the Potomac. He was in charge of the construction and operation of the huge supply depot at City Point, strategically located at the confluence of the James and Appomattox rivers. Some two hundred or more ships arrived daily during the war, and, in the amazingly short time of about forty days, this obscure, backwater town was transformed into one of the busiest ports in the world. It became the staging ground for the massive Siege of Petersburg, which led to the eventual Confederate surrender at Appomattox. *(May 1865. Photographer unknown.)*

Brigadier General John A. Rawlins with his wife and child at their quarters in City Point, Virginia. Rawlins joined the U.S. Army as a captain under Grant's command and remained with the general throughout the war. He was known for his great attention to detail, as well as being a perfectionist in proper protocol. When Grant was promoted to general-in-chief of all Union armies, Rawlins became his chief of staff of the U.S. Army General Headquarters. *(Date and photographer unknown.)*

A pontoon bridge over the James River near Jones Landing, Virginia, left. Upon finding many bridges destroyed by Confederate troops, Union engineering units constructed temporary floating bridges across major rivers and streams. The floating pontoons and road surface were lashed together so that the bridge could flex under a load, and the component parts could be dismantled easily, moved to another location, and reassembled where needed. *(Date and photographer unknown.)*

The locomotive "Governor Nye" at City Point, Virginia. When General Grant began the Siege of Petersburg, he set up an enormous rail depot at City Point from which to supply his army. Over a mile and a half of wharves were constructed, along with new warehouses and other buildings. The railroad terminal, with twenty-five engines and almost three hundred boxcars, was able to transport fifteen hundred tons of supplies a day to the siege-lines at Petersburg, eight miles away. *(Date and photographer unknown.)*

A group of Federal officers at City Point, Virginia. City Point was the Union's advance supply depot, situated deep in the heart of the Confederacy, only twenty miles from the Southern capital of Richmond. From the end of June 1864 to May 1865, City Point provided all necessary supplies to support General Grant's armies as they lay siege to the strategically important town of Petersburg, Virginia. *(Date and photographer unknown.)*

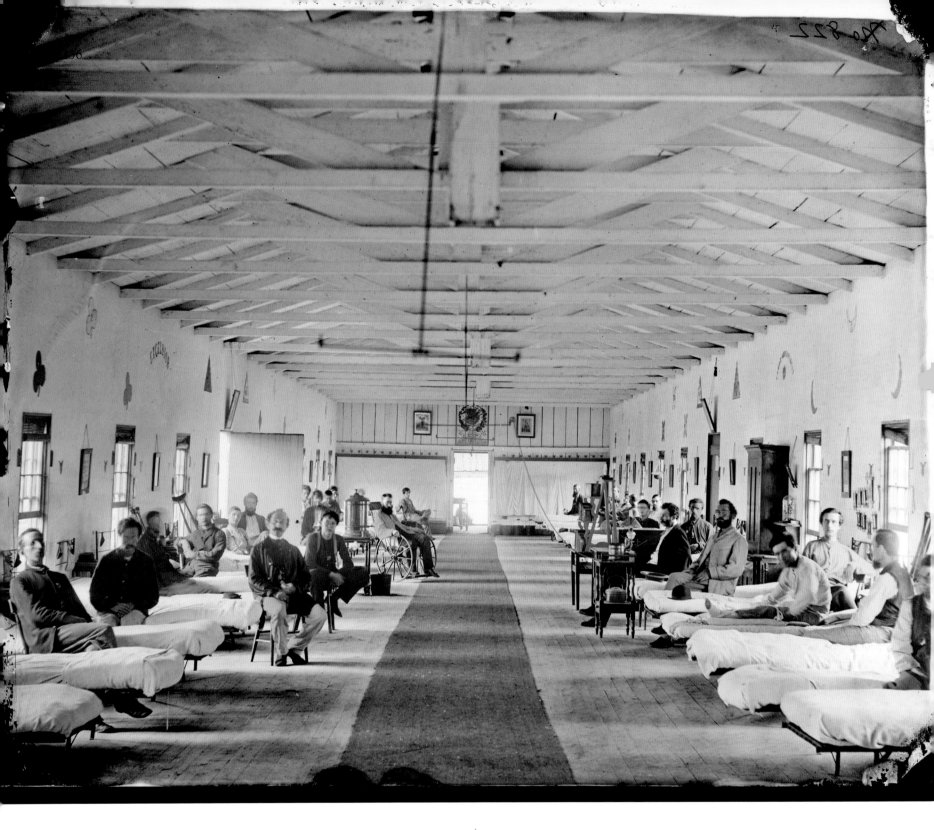

Patients in Ward K of the Armory Square Hospital at Washington, D.C. Constructed in 1862, this medical facility was named after the adjacent District of Columbia Armory. The one thousand-bed complex of twelve pavilions and overflow tents was one of the largest Civil War hospitals and was located where the Smithsonian's National Air and Space Museum stands today.

After early Union defeats, Washington became crowded with wounded soldiers. The military soon realized that existing facilities were inadequate, so public buildings were converted into hospitals. These facilities were hospitals in name only. In addition to sanitary deficiencies, food given to patients was no better than what they had received on the battlefield. *(August 1865. Photographer unknown.)*

An enlarged detail of a group of Union soldiers and the medical supply boat *Planter* at General Hospital wharf on the Appomattox River near City Point, Virginia. This location was about a mile north of City Point, the supply base for Union forces at Petersburg. *Planter* was part of the fleet serving the Union medical department. The ship, which was built in 1860 at Charleston, South Carolina, was originally an armed transport vessel for the Confederacy. On May 13, 1862, Robert Smalls, a slave who was pilot of the *Planter,* commandeered the ship while her captain was ashore. He steamed past Confederate strongholds, including Fort Sumter, and when out of range lowered the Confederate flag and surrendered the vessel to a Union blockade ship. Newspaper stories telling of his heroic deed made Smalls famous throughout the North. President Lincoln signed a congressional bill rewarding him and his two African American crewmen one-half the value of *Planter* as prize money. Because of his broad knowledge of Confederate defenses and shipyards, Smalls was able to provide valuable assistance to the Union navy, and in December 1863, he became the first African American captain of a U.S. vessel. *(Date and photographer unknown.)*

The wagons and camera of Sam A. Cooley, photographer, Department of the South. Samuel A. Cooley was attached to the 10th U.S. Army Corps as their official photographer and recorded the happenings around Savannah, Fort McAllister, Jacksonville, St. Augustine, Beaufort, and Charleston. He also operated a studio in Beaufort, South Carolina, and documented the area after the invasion of the southern coast in the autumn of 1862. (*Date and photographer unknown.*)

☛ A closer view of photographer Sam Cooley and associates. Civil War–era photographs were made on light-sensitized glass plates sized to fit a specific camera. Positive prints were then directly printed onto albumen paper. Many cameras of the time period produced stereo negatives, which recorded left and right images using twin lenses. Those negatives were generally four by ten inches in size, and a nonstereo print from those plates would yield a photo half that size. Enlargements were not practical to produce, so a larger photograph required a larger camera and glass plate (Mathew Brady produced "Imperial" images using mammoth seventeen- by twenty-inch negatives). The camera shown here appears to be quite a bit larger as evidenced by the size of the plate holder in the hand of the assistant, possibly eleven by fourteen inches.

A Zouave ambulance crew demonstrating the removal of wounded soldiers from the battlefield. In August 1862, General George McClellan created an Ambulance Corps for the Army of the Potomac. Prior to that, the most unfit soldiers were often given that detail, and they were usually little better as medical assistants. McClellan's improved system for removing wounded from the battlefield was copied by other field armies, although it was not until March 1864 that Congress passed an act to create an Ambulance Corps for all Union armies. This staged photograph illustrates a number of services the crew might be called upon to render: bandaging and offering water to a wounded soldier, carrying a casualty from battle on a litter, and placing an injured person into the ambulance for transport to the field hospital. Note the wooden splint on the soldier in the ambulance, as well as the officer pretending to direct his men. *(Date and photographer unknown.)*

An obviously staged and somewhat humorous photograph that was made at a Union army winter quarters. (*Date, location, and photographer unknown.*)

Sunday morning mass at the camp of the 69th
New York State Militia. Regimental chaplains
were to be provided for the regular army by a War
Department act of August 3, 1861. It is estimated that
as many as three thousand chaplains became part of
the Union forces following that decree. In addition
to Protestant ministers and Roman Catholic priests,
the war also saw the appointment of the first Jewish
and the first African American chaplains into service.
The most important duties of chaplains were the
worship services they conducted in tents, outdoors,
or around campfires. They also offered comfort and
support during troubled times and even helped write
letters home for soldiers unable to do so. Notice that
women are also in attendance at this service.
(Date and photographer unknown.)

4

WAR MACHINES

66 The dogmas of the quiet past are inadequate to the stormy present. The occasion is piled high with difficulty, and we must rise with the occasion. As our case is new, so we must think anew and act anew. We must disenthrall ourselves, and then we shall save our country. 99

Abraham Lincoln

Some writers have called the Civil War the last of the ancient wars and first of the modern wars because it combined technological improvements with ancient brute force. So-called "edged weapons"—which included swords, bayonets, sabers, and lances—were occasionally used in battle, but they primarily served decorative purposes, indicating a military officer's authority. The primary exception to this was the cavalry sword, or saber, which was indeed a legitimate weapon in the hands of trained cavalry troops.

Civil War small arms consisted of pistol and revolver handguns, muskets, long-barrel rifles, and shorter barrel carbines with both rifled and smoothbore barrels. Rifling is the process of machining circular grooves inside the barrel of a firearm, which causes a projectile to spin

as it is propelled along the length of the barrel. The spin gyroscopically stabilizes the bullet during flight, improving its stability and accuracy. The introduction of rifled barrels greatly increased the precision, range, and deadliness of the weapons used in the Civil War. The primary small arms for both the Northern and Southern armies were the .58 caliber Springfield musket and the .69 caliber Harpers Ferry rifle. Both of these were muzzle-loading arms with rifled barrels that fired deadly minié balls, which were actually bullet shaped and not round balls.

Civil War cannon were categorized based upon size, barrel length, and projectile weight. The guns were then further designated for use on the field, in garrisons, or on ships. The most popular field guns—and the ones most people think of when they envision Civil War-era cannon—were the smoothbore artillery pieces called "Napoleons." Developed in France in 1853 and named after its emperor at the time, Napoleon III, these were cast using bronze or iron smoothbore and fired twelve-pound projectiles up to sixteen hundred yards. Other cannon included Parrott, Blakely, and Brooke rifles, as well as Dahlgren guns. Parrott rifles, named after West Point graduate and inventor Robert Parker Parrott, were made in sizes ranging from ten-pounders (meaning it could launch a cannonball weighing ten pounds) to the rare three-hundred-pounders. Both the Northern and Southern armies used ten- and twenty-pounder versions on the battlefield, with the twenty- pounder being the largest field gun used during the war. Its barrel weighed over eighteen hundred pounds and its range approached two thousand yards. The much larger one hundred–pound naval version could fire its shell almost four miles. Although quite accurate and also cheaper to make than most rifled artillery guns, Parrott rifles were generally disliked by most officers because of their poor safety reputation.

Blakely rifles were muzzle-loading cannon with rifled barrels designed by Captain Theophilus Blakely, a British army officer. When Blakely failed to interest the British government in his designs, he began selling cannon to the Confederacy. They ranged from six-pounders to four hundred fifty-pounders. One famous Blakely rifle was the "Widow Blakely." On May 22, 1863, this 7 1/2-inch rifle was being used by Confederates defending Vicksburg, Mississippi, when a shell exploded in the gun's barrel. The explosion ripped off the end of the muzzle, so the Confederate gun crew cut two feet off the barrel and continued using the gun as a mortar for the duration of the battle.

Brooke rifles were designed by John Mercer Brooke, a Confederate naval officer. During the war, Tredegar Iron Works in Richmond, Virginia, and the Naval Ordnance Works in Selma, Alabama, made 6 1/2-, 7-, and 8-inch rifled versions, as well as 10- and 11-inch smoothbore versions. These guns were mounted both on Confederate ships and on shore in coastal defense batteries manned by the Rebels.

All of the above artillery weapons could fire solid projectiles, as well as explosive shells. Essentially antipersonnel weapons, these shells were hollow castings filled with black powder, which acted as a burst charge when ignited by a variable-timed fuse. When detonated, the powder charge burst the shells into hundreds of pieces of shrapnel.

Dahlgren guns were muzzle-loading artillery pieces designed by John A. Dahlgren of the U.S. Navy. Dahlgren initially designed bronze-cast twelve- and twenty-pound smoothbore boat howitzers (a howitzer is a short-barrel gun that shoots projectiles at high angles with a small amount of powder). These guns were actually designed to be used on smaller military boats, but they were placed on most Federal naval vessels during the war. By the end of the Civil War, Dahlgren had developed a range of naval guns with rifled barrels in sizes up to twenty inches. These larger guns fired shells in varying weights, from thirty pounds to more than three hundred pounds. His design called for a gun casting with a smooth, curved shape that concentrated most of the metal in the breech of the gun, which sustained the greatest detonation force. The efficacy of the design was proven, as no Dahlgren gun exploded while in service— quite unusual for artillery of that period. All of the larger Dahlgren guns were made of cast iron and had a distinctive shape that caused them to be nicknamed "soda bottles."

Mortars were stubby guns, designed to lob explosive shells high into the air that would then fall either over fortification walls, in the case of siege mortars, or above the heads of infantry, in the case of field mortars. Smaller mortars were able to be moved by two or three men and ☞

fired shells weighing 17 or 44 pounds. Larger siege mortars fired shells that weighed 88 and 200 pounds respectively. Probably the best known Union mortar was the "Dictator," a thirteen-inch seacoast mortar weighing 17,000 pounds, mounted atop a reinforced railroad car. It was used during the siege of Vicksburg and was able to throw a 200-pound explosive shell a distance of $2^1/_2$ miles. Confederate forces used mortars as well, although none were as large as the Dictator.

The destructiveness of Civil War artillery was substantial. Shells of various types were employed for specific purposes. Solid shot was a round, cast-iron projectile with no internal explosive charge—what could be considered a typical cannon ball. It caused damage by directly impacting buildings and other targets. A shell was an elongated hollow casting with an internal explosive charge detonated by either a timed fuse or a percussion fuse that exploded upon impact. Shells loaded only with gunpowder were called common shells. Canisters filled with iron balls, bullet slugs, or even scrap metal and then stuffed with sawdust and sealed were called canister or case shot. Grapeshot consisted of a wooden base plate with a long center bolt around which larger metal balls were arranged and held together using a canvas and rope covering. These deadly shells were used as antipersonnel weapons and essentially turned a cannon into a large shotgun with devastating results.

Another significant advance in warfare was the use of ironclad warships. On April 19, 1861, President Lincoln announced a blockade of Confederate port cities on the Atlantic and Gulf coasts to try to prevent the movement of Confederate supplies and arms. Over time, this Union blockade became a powerful and effective weapon against the Southern economy. In an attempt to overcome the blockade, the South salvaged the USS *Merrimack* a sunken steam-powered, wooden frigate that had been scuttled by the U.S. Navy rather than let her fall into enemy hands. The Confederacy converted her into an ironclad warship, rechristened the CSS *Virginia*. Hearing of this, the U.S. Navy built three ironclads in response, the first being the USS *Monitor*.

In early March of 1862, the arrival in the James River of the CSS *Virginia*, still called the *Merrimack* by some, threatened the Union blockade and caused the Union navy to bring in the USS *Monitor*. The resulting clash became known as the Battle of Hampton Roads and was the first ever combat between ironclad ships. The battle, which lasted for two days, was essentially a draw, yet the encounter was immediately noticed by navies around the world as a harbinger of naval battles to come with this new type of warship. Neither ship ever fought again after the battle as they were both eventually sunk: the CSS *Virginia* in the James River during an attempt to move her to Richmond and the USS *Monitor* in the Atlantic Ocean while being towed to Beaufort, North Carolina. Eventually the word "monitor" became a general term for a Federal class of ironclad warships. ❖

Columbiad guns of the Confederate water battery at Warrington, Florida (the entrance to Pensacola Bay). The Columbiad was a large-caliber, smoothbore cannon able to fire heavy shot or shells for long ranges, making it an excellent seacoast defense weapon. *(February 1861. Photographer unknown.)*

Thirteen-inch seacoast mortars of Federal Battery No. 4 with officers of the 1st Connecticut Heavy Artillery Unit, Yorktown, Virginia. The Battle (or Siege) of Yorktown took place near the site of the American Revolutionary War battle of the same name. Union general George McClellan planned to surround and capture Yorktown on the Virginia peninsula with Federal navy forces as well as ground troops. His amphibious plan went awry with the appearance of the Confederate ironclad ship, CSS *Virginia*. He then set about constructing artillery installations of massive seacoast mortars in order to lay siege to Yorktown. *(May 1862. James F. Gibson, photographer.)*

A gun that fired one-hundred-pound shells mounted on the
Confederate gunboat CSS *Teaser*. While engaging USS *Maratanza*
on the James River on July 4, 1862, a Union shell blew up the
boiler on CSS *Teaser* and forced her crew to abandon ship.
(July 4, 1862. James F. Gibson, photographer.)

U.S. Navy officers on the deck of the ironclad ship USS *Monitor* on the
James River in Virginia. This photograph was taken exactly four months after her historic
battle with CSS *Virginia* in the Battle of Hampton Roads on March 9, 1862. Note the
cannonball damage to the turret. *(July 9, 1862. James F. Gibson, photographer.)*

Union sailors relaxing and playing checkers on the deck of the USS *Monitor* on the James River, Virginia. Sixty-three crew members ran the *Monitor*: seven officers and fifty-six sailors. The crew felt a proud camaraderie and began referring to themselves as "Monitor Boys." Because of the scarcity of native seamen, many of the crewmen came from northern Europe, particularly Ireland and Scandinavia. During the war, almost one-quarter of enlisted Union sailors were foreign-born. (*July 9, 1862. James F. Gibson, photographer.*)

Haas & Peale.

A 300-pound Parrott rifle at Morris Island, South Carolina. This is one of the three 10-inch Parrott rifles located on Morris Island, South Carolina. One of the largest rifled artillery pieces in use during the Civil War, the 10-inch Parrott could fire a 250-pound explosive projectile a distance of nine thousand yards. This gun lost 18 inches off its muzzle when a round prematurely exploded inside the barrel. Union troops filed the ragged edges down and kept this battery in action with little ill effect. *(July or August 1863. Haas and Peale, photographers.)*

U.S. Navy rear admiral John A. Dahlgren standing beside a fifty-pound Dahlgren rifle, one of the bottle-shaped, cast-iron cannons he designed. The photo was taken aboard USS *Pawnee* in Charleston Harbor, South Carolina, circa 1863–65, while he was commanding the South Atlantic blockading squadron. *(Date and photographer unknown.)*

A Federal ammunition magazine and stacked cannon shells at Battery Rodgers in Alexandria, Virginia. This site was an important part of Civil War defenses for Washington, D.C. Located on a high cliff, its position afforded a clear line of fire on the southern Potomac River as well as Fort Hunt Road which were two possible approaches of invasion. The guns were supplied by two adjacent powder magazines, one of which is seen here. The battery was garrisoned by six commissioned officers, one ordnance sergeant, and two hundred fifty-six men. (*Date unknown. William Frank Browne, photographer.*)

Another view of Battery Rodgers at the confluence of Hunting Creek and the Potomac River in Alexandria, Virginia. An eight-inch Parrott rifle that fired two hundred-pound shells stands in the foreground, with a fifteen-inch Rodman gun beyond it. The Rodman was one of the largest guns in the world at that time. Note the iron tracks for rotating the guns. (*Date and photographer unknown.*)

A railroad gun, with its crew, used during the Siege of Petersburg, Virginia. Here a Federal Parrott rifle is mounted on a railroad flatcar with an iron and wooden shield to deflect counter fire. Mounting large guns to railroad cars was a technological improvement devised during the Civil War that allowed quicker and easier movement of heavy artillery pieces. A gun crew was able to move their weapon to a desirable place and immediately fire it; recoil pushed the weapon back along the tracks, where it was slowed by ropes. The gun was then reloaded and pushed again into firing position. *(1864 or 1865. Photographer unknown.)*

A 15-inch Federal Rodman gun used to defend Washington, D.C. This huge smoothbore gun was able to fire spherical shot, as well as shells, and weighed almost 50,000 pounds. It used a 40-pound powder charge to shoot a 300-pound shell more than two miles. *(August 1864. Photographer unknown.)*

A battery of Parrott rifles manned by Company C,
1st Connecticut Heavy Artillery at Fort Brady, Virginia.
Note the rounds of ammunition carefully stacked against the
fortification walls. *(1864. Photographer unknown.)*

☞ A closer view of a gun crew proudly
posing for a photograph. Company C,
1st Connecticut Heavy Artillery at Fort
Brady, Virginia.

"The Dictator" at Petersburg, Virginia.
One of the largest Civil War guns, the Dictator
was a 13-inch seacoast mortar made of cast iron.
Weighing more than 17,000 pounds and fired
from a reinforced railway flatcar, it used 20 pounds
of gunpowder per shot to throw the 218-pound
explosive shells a distance of two to three miles,
depending on barrel elevation. *(September 1864.
David Knox, photographer.)*

The men of Company G, 1st Connecticut Heavy Artillery manned "the Dictator" during its use at the
Siege of Petersburg. A curved sidetrack extending from the main railroad line was constructed especially for
the huge mortar; the curve in the tracks allowed the Dictator's gun crew to adjust the direction of fire.

The twin-turreted monitor USS *Onondaga*, with Union soldiers manning the oars of a rowboat on the James River, Virginia, in the foreground. The *Onondaga* was somewhat unique in that her hull was constructed entirely from iron, instead of metal plating over a wooden hull. She was built at the Continental Iron Works in Greenpoint, New York, and was launched on July 29, 1863. Commanded by Captain Melancton Smith, the *Onondaga* arrived at Hampton Roads, Virginia, on April 23, 1864, and operated primarily in the James River Flotilla. She supported General Grant's drive to Richmond, which subsequently brought the war to a close. She was decommissioned in New York City on June 8, 1865. Following the war, the *Onondaga* was sold to France, where she had a long career with the French navy, and was finally sold for scrap in 1904. *(1864. Photographer unknown.)*

A seven-inch rifled Brooke gun at a Confederate gun emplacement overlooking the James River in Virginia. The battery was built in May 1864 to prevent the Federal army from using the James River to approach Richmond. (April 1865. Photographer unknown.)

Captured siege guns at Rocketts Landing in Richmond, Virginia. Rocketts Landing was a small community on the James River. Due to its location, it was vital to the defense of Richmond from naval attack and became part of the Confederate navy yard. On April 2, 1865, the navy yard and its ships burned in the fire that destroyed the Confederate capital. Two days later, Abraham Lincoln came ashore at Rocketts Landing to tour the city, still smoldering in the distance. *(1865. Photographer unknown.)*

☞ A closer view at Rocketts Landing, which was originally the site of a James River ferry crossing operated by Robert Rocketts in the early 1700s. It eventually grew into a riverfront town and, at one point, was one of the busiest inland ports in North America.

Another Confederate seven-inch Brooke rifle overlooking the James River in Virginia near Trent's Reach. These guns were muzzle-loading naval and coastal defense weapons designed by John Mercer Brooke, an officer in the Confederate navy. *(April 1865. Photographer unknown.)*

A heavy gun mounted on the inner line of Confederate defense fortifications at Petersburg, Virginia. Petersburg, a heavily fortified Confederate city about twenty miles south of Richmond, played a major part in the defense of the Confederate capital. In an attempt to capture Richmond, Union forces under General Grant laid siege to Petersburg for nine months. *(April 3, 1865. Photographer unknown.)*

Officers posing on the deck of the USS *Catskill*, with Lieutenant Commander Edward Barrett seated on the turret, while the ship was in Charleston Harbor, South Carolina. On either side of the turret are the ship's two Dahlgren twelve-pound deck howitzers. The *Catskill* was launched on December 16, 1862, in Greenpoint, New York, and she continued to serve the navy after the end of the Civil War. She was finally decommissioned in 1898, following the Spanish-American War. *(1865. Photographer unknown.)*

A **Confederate gun emplacement** above Dutch Gap on the James River in Virginia. This is typical of the heavily fortified gun emplacements the Confederacy constructed overlooking the James River to protect Richmond. *(April 1865. Photographer unknown.)*

A **"powder monkey"** standing by a gun aboard the USS *New Hampshire* off the coast of Charleston, South Carolina. "Powder monkey" was a Civil War term for boys quick and agile enough to keep gun crews supplied with gunpowder and shot. Their job was to run bags of powder from stores below decks to the gun crew in times of battle. At other times they did menial tasks, earning little more than food and a place to sleep. They were given the rank of "boy," a Civil War-era naval rank just below private. Contrabands who fled to Union lines were also allowed to enlist at the rank of boy at half pay. There is a record of one boy who was still serving well into his forties. *(1864 or 1865. Photographer unknown.)*

5

DESTRUCTION

"A house divided against itself cannot stand.'
I believe this government cannot endure, permanently, half slave and half free.
I do not expect the Union to be dissolved; I do not expect the house to fall;
but I do expect it will cease to be divided.
It will become all one thing, or all the other."

Abraham Lincoln

On April 12, 1861, when Confederate artillery shelled the Union's Fort Sumter in Charleston Harbor, few could have then imagined that the war would continue for almost five years and be the cause of massive destruction and nationwide chaos. The Civil War was arguably the most significant disruption of American lives in the history of the Republic, with a cost of 6.5 billion dollars in national treasure (in 1860s valuation), as well as the loss of an estimated 625 thousand American lives. The destruction from the war was overwhelming—the following photographs display the effectiveness of Civil War–era artillery, as well as the results of the many fires that ravaged the South during the conflict.

In the mid-eighteenth century, Robert Harper established a ferry boat service at the confluence of the Potomac and Shenandoah rivers. His ferry allowed pioneers to reach their destinations in the newly opened land to the west, and the settlement grew in size as a transportation hub. Because of the abundant water power to run machinery, the United States government purchased 125 acres of land from Harper's heirs in 1796 to build a national armory there. Construction of the U.S. Armory and Arsenal at Harpers Ferry began three years later; by 1810, arms production averaged about ten thousand pieces annually. By the start of the Civil War the armory had become one of the leading weapon makers in the country. Consequently, when Virginia seceded from the Union, the armory became a desirable target for the Confederacy.

On April 18, 1861, just a day after Virginia's secession, Union soldiers set fire to their own Harpers

Ferry arsenal and armory in an attempt to thwart its capture by a very small advancing Confederate militia. Several arsenal buildings and fifteen thousand weapons were destroyed by Union soldiers before local Harpers Ferry residents—many of whom made their living working in the arsenal—swiftly extinguished the fires. The Confederate army then rescued much of the armory's weapon-making machinery and shipped it south. After confiscating what was left in the arsenal, Southern forces resumed the destruction of the facility by burning the remaining armory buildings to the ground, at which point the destruction was total.

Based on 1860 census numbers, the city of Charleston, South Carolina, was the twenty-second largest city in the United States and had a population of more than forty thousand people when the war began. It was an important Atlantic Ocean port city, and a center of the Confederate secessionist movement. Many Southern ports had been closed by the Union blockade imposed by President Lincoln right after the war began, and Charleston became one of the leading Southern ports for blockade runners. It was also a major site of conflict and combat throughout the war. Although the city and its surrounding fortifications were repeatedly targeted by the Union army and navy, numerous attempts to take Charleston or destroy its defenses at first proved futile. With the development of longer range and more accurate artillery and the ability of Union forces to place batteries closer to the city on Morris Island, a year-long Federal artillery barrage began in late 1863 that severely damaged much of Charleston.

Subsequent Union assaults finally forced the Confederate army to abandon the city on February 15, 1865, when Union general William T. Sherman threatened to raze the city during his "March to the Sea." In May 1865, Sherman toured the city, proclaiming, "Any one who is not *satisfied* with war, should go and see Charleston, and he will pray louder and deeper than ever that the country may, in the long future, be spared any more war." Although Charleston did not fall to Federal forces until the final months of the war, nevertheless it was nearly destroyed by fire and bombardment and was a ghost town by the war's end.

Richmond, Virginia, was another Southern city heavily damaged by the Civil War. The 1860 census listed the population of Richmond as almost thirty-eight thousand people, slightly smaller than Charleston. In addition to being the capital of the Confederate States of America, Richmond was a vital source of manpower, supplies, and weapons for the Confederacy. The city's huge Tredegar Iron Works manufactured railroad locomotives and munitions, including about half of the South's total artillery production during the war. The foundry also made the armor plating that covered the CSS *Virginia*, rebuilt from the USS *Merrimack*, which fought the first battle between ironclad warships in 1862.

Throughout the war, Richmond was the target of many assaults by Union forces attempting to capture the city, but its defenses held. In 1864, Union general Ulysses S. Grant's Richmond-Petersburg Campaign laid siege to neighboring Petersburg, Virginia, whose numerous railroads were a lifeline to Richmond. The 292-day siege was aimed at strangling Richmond.

Following successful Union attacks on April 1 and 2, 1865, Confederate general Robert E. Lee abandoned Petersburg and headed south in an attempt to join up with General Joseph Johnston's army in North Carolina. President Jefferson Davis and his cabinet abandoned Richmond the same day and fled south on the last open railroad line to Danville, Virginia, where they hoped to set up a temporary government. Retreating Confederate soldiers were under orders to set fire to bridges, supply warehouses, and the armory as they evacuated the Confederate capital. The resulting fires raged out of control in the largely abandoned city, destroying major parts of Richmond. The fire burned until the following day, Monday, April 3, when it was finally extinguished by the Union troops streaming into the city. Noted photographer Alexander Gardner was able to thoroughly document the desolate and devastated Confederate capital shortly after the evacuation. Some of those remarkable photographs are shown here. ❖

Ruins of the Harpers Ferry arsenal at Harpers Ferry, West Virginia. When the war began in April 1861, the original Federal defenders torched the facility in order to prevent it from falling into enemy hands. Confederates then overran the facility to confiscate the remaining weapon-making machinery, which was shipped farther south. Within two weeks, Confederates again burned the remaining buildings to the ground, leaving it a worthless ruin. *(October 1862. D. B. Woodbury, photographer.)*

Part of the destruction along the James River and Kanawha Canal near the Haxall Flour Mills in Richmond, Virginia. The ruins of the Gallego Mills are seen beyond. Uncontrolled fires set by fleeing Confederate troops as they relinquished and abandoned the Southern capital caused utter devastation to a large part of the city. *(1865. Photographer unknown.)*

A burned locomotive among the ruins of the Richmond and Petersburg railroad depot in Richmond, Virginia. The destruction resulted from fires that burned out of control after the Confederate government and troops left Richmond, Virginia. Union troops helped extinguish the fires when they arrived the following day. *(1865. Photographer unknown.)*

Another view of destroyed buildings in the burned district of Richmond, Virginia, at the end of the Civil War. *(1865. Photographer unknown.)*

The ruins of a paper mill, with wrecked papermaking machinery in the foreground, at Richmond, Virginia. Because of its location on the James River, Richmond was able to use water to power many of its large industries, such as flour and paper mills, which were driven by huge water wheels. This paper mill was destroyed by the great fire that leveled much of Richmond during the Confederate evacuation of the city. *(April 1865. Alexander Gardner, photographer.)*

A view of many ruined buildings through the porch of the Circular Church at 150 Meeting Street in Charleston, South Carolina. The Circular Congregational Church is one of the oldest continuously operating houses of worship in the South, and the graveyard behind the church is the city's oldest. The church wreckage shown here was further damaged by an earthquake in 1886. Six years later, the building was rebuilt using most of the original bricks. It still stands today.
(April 1865. George Barnard, photographer.)

A closer view of four African American children playing in the ruins of Charleston, South Carolina. Note that they are barefoot despite all the debris.

The house of Michael O'Connor at 180 Broad
Street in Charleston, South Carolina, with remains of
another house in the foreground. During the last months
of the war, the O'Connor house was used to hold Union
officers captured by the Confederacy. (April 1865.
George Barnard, photographer.)

☞ A closer view of bystanders among heavily
battered buildings of Charleston. It was common
practice for Civil War photographers to include
people in many of their pictures of otherwise
sterile compositions, even though their poses are
often stiff or a bit contrived.

A view of the burned district in Richmond, Virginia, with the capitol building still standing across the Canal Basin. During the chaotic evacuation of Richmond on April 2, 1865, Confederate troops burned tobacco warehouses in the commercial and industrial districts, in advance of the Union troops entering the city, causing incredible devastation, in addition to widespread looting. Note the massive pile of deserted Confederate guns and ammunition in the foreground. (1865. *Photographer unknown.*)

Chimneys stand alone amid massive destruction in the burned area of Richmond, Virginia. This photograph thoroughly illustrates the level of complete destruction suffered by the largest Southern cities following the war. *(April 1865. Photographer unknown.)*

6

LINCOLN

> **"** Incontestably the greatest man I ever knew. **"**

It is somewhat ironic that Abraham Lincoln's presidency is defined by the American Civil War even though he personally had very little prior military experience. For about three months in 1832, Lincoln had been a member of the Illinois state militia during the Black Hawk War, a Native American uprising. As a captain, Lincoln was elected to be his company's commander, although he never saw combat during his tour of duty.

Years later, as Lincoln's election to the presidency became more probable, Southern secessionists pushed to leave the Union if Lincoln became president. Lincoln won the election on November 6, 1860, and South Carolina declared its secession on December 20. A month and a half later, Mississippi, Florida, Alabama, Georgia, Louisiana, and Texas followed. State militias in these seceding states began to confiscate Federal forts, as well as armaments at Federal arsenals.

Inauguration Day—March 4, 1860—started out overcast, and the crowd began arriving at dawn at the new and only partially constructed Capitol building, where Lincoln's address and swearing-in would take place. By noon the sun had broken through the clouds, and the crowd had grown to about forty thousand people. Security was extremely heavy, with more than twenty-five hundred members of the military supplementing local police, while plainclothes detectives mingled with the crowd.

Shortly after one in the afternoon, Lincoln arrived by carriage, accompanied by outgoing president James Buchanan, and was introduced to the crowd by his long-time friend, Senator Edward Baker of Oregon.

Lincoln began his inaugural address by reassuring the South that he did not intend to interfere with slavery in the states where it then existed. After these assurances, however, Lincoln declared, "Plainly, the central idea of secession is the essence of anarchy." It was his duty, as he saw it, to "hold, occupy, and possess the property and places belonging to the government." Further, Lincoln stated, "We are not enemies, but friends. We must not be enemies. Though passion may have strained, it must not break our bonds of affection."

As Lincoln assumed the office of president, an informal and uneasy truce settled upon the country. It lasted less than six weeks, torn asunder by the firing on Fort Sumter.

Lincoln scholar Allan Nevins has suggested that Lincoln made three important mistakes at the beginning of the war: He underestimated the strength of the Confederacy, believing that seventy-five thousand Federal troops could quell the insurrection in three months; he overestimated sentiment for the Union in Southern and border states; and he failed to understand that Unionists in border states would not support invading the Confederacy.

Lincoln took an active part in planning the war despite his lack of military experience. He expected to guarantee adequate defenses of the national capital and to carry out the war in an uncompromising manner in order to quickly bring it to an end. Lincoln had a contentious and difficult relationship with a number of his eastern theater generals early in the war and decided to promote General Ulysses S. Grant following his numerous victories in the western theater, including Vicksburg and Chattanooga. Lincoln was so impressed by Grant, he once said of him, "I cannot spare this man. He fights." Investing his faith in the new commanding general, Lincoln authorized Grant to destroy the Confederacy's infrastructure, hoping to destroy the South's morale and weaken its ability to continue the war. Grant's aggressive campaign eventually bottled up Lee in the Siege of Petersburg, took Richmond, and brought the war to a close in the spring of 1865.

Throughout the war, President Lincoln avidly followed telegraph reports of news from his generals sent from the various sites of battle via field telegraph units. On fifteen occasions, he personally visited his generals at the battlefields to evaluate the progress of the war, inspire them before battles, and reassure them after setbacks. His first trip was on July 23, 1861, immediately following the First Battle of Bull Run, a sizeable Confederate victory. The resulting Federal retreat rapidly deteriorated into a rout as the shattered Union army fled for the safety of Washington. His final visit to the field was in April 1865, immediately following the fall of Richmond. During the battle, President Lincoln had been staying nearby at City Point, Virginia, which was the headquarters of the Union army during the Siege of Petersburg. After the city's evacuation, he toured the destroyed city on foot with his young son Tad, saw the Virginia State Capitol, and visited the former White House of the Confederacy, where he reportedly sat in Jefferson Davis's chair.

Civil War photographer Alexander Gardner took his famous photographs of President Lincoln with his generals during Lincoln's visit on October 3, 1862, to Sharpsburg, Maryland, after the Battle of Antietam (seen on pages 194–201). ❖

Intelligence agent Allan Pinkerton, President Lincoln, and Major General John A. McClernand at Sharpsburg, Maryland, two weeks after the Battle of Antietam. Originally a deputy sheriff in Chicago, Pinkerton formed his own company, the Pinkerton Detective Agency, in 1852. It was the first such agency in the United States. By solving a series of train robberies, Pinkerton's agency became a major success. On the front of his three-story Chicago headquarters was a large sign bearing the company's slogan, "We Never Sleep," below a huge, black-and-white eye. This Pinkerton logo originated the term "private eye." (*October 3, 1862. Alexander Gardner, photographer.*)

☞ A closer view of the three men. In 1861, the Pinkerton Agency was assigned to guard Lincoln following his election to the presidency. While in Baltimore, on the way to the inauguration, Pinkerton foiled an assassination plot. Following this, General George McClellan tapped Pinkerton to organize a "secret" intelligence service for the Army of the Potomac. Pinkerton remained a civilian, but under the alias Major E. J. Allen he gathered intelligence and oversaw a team of sixteen to eighteen agents.

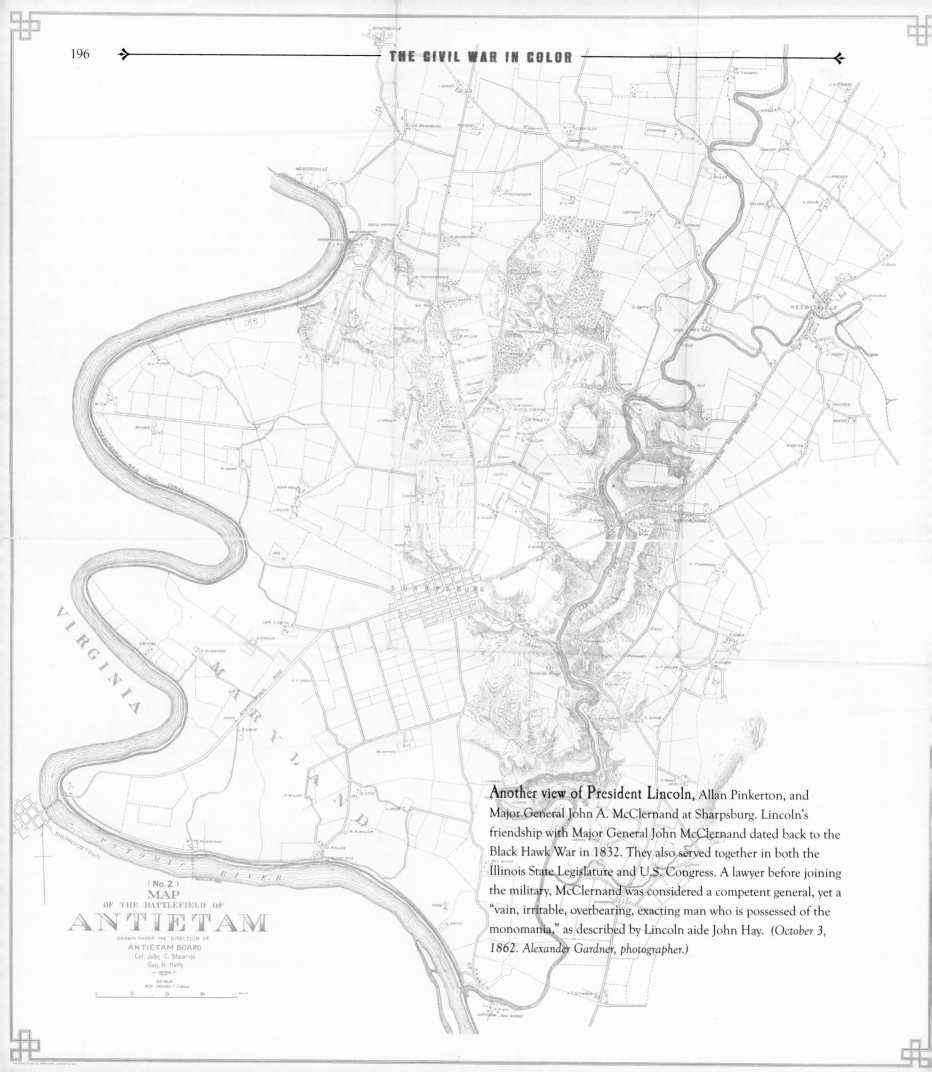

(No. 2)
MAP
OF THE BATTLEFIELD OF
ANTIETAM
DRAWN UNDER THE DIRECTION OF
ANTIETAM BOARD
Col. John C. Stearns.
Gen. H. Heth.
—1894—
SCALE
4¼ INCHES = 1 MILE

Another view of President Lincoln, Allan Pinkerton, and Major General John A. McClernand at Sharpsburg. Lincoln's friendship with Major General John McClernand dated back to the Black Hawk War in 1832. They also served together in both the Illinois State Legislature and U.S. Congress. A lawyer before joining the military, McClernand was considered a competent general, yet a "vain, irritable, overbearing, exacting man who is possessed of the monomania," as described by Lincoln aide John Hay. *(October 3, 1862. Alexander Gardner, photographer.)*

President Lincoln and General George B. McClellan in the general's tent at Sharpsburg. General McClellan was one of the most popular of Civil War commanders with his soldiers, but his cautious leadership during and following the Battle of Antietam allowed Lee's army to resist defeat despite being outnumbered. After the two sides improvised a truce to allow the recovery and exchange of the wounded, Lee's forces began withdrawing. Lincoln was incensed that McClellan did not pursue Lee's forces across the Potomac to ensure a Union victory. *(October 3, 1862. Alexander Gardner, photographer.)*

☞ A closer view of Lincoln and McClellen. Despite Lincoln's well-known evaluation of General McClellan— "If he can't fight himself, he excels in making others ready to fight"—when McClellan failed to pursue Lee's forces after Antietam, the president removed him from command, thus ending the general's military career. McClellan later became the unsuccessful Democratic nominee opposing Lincoln in the 1864 presidential election.

President Lincoln with his generals at Sharpsburg. The Battle of Antietam was the single bloodiest day of the Civil War—2,100 Union soldiers were killed and 9,500 wounded; 1,500 Confederates were killed and 7,750 wounded. Around 39,000 Southerners fought against 75,000 Union soldiers and, in spite of being outnumbered two-to-one, Lee's army was able to meet each Federal challenge. Although the battle had no clear winner, General George McClellan was considered the victor because General Robert E. Lee withdrew to Virginia. *(October 3, 1862. Alexander Gardner, photographer.)*

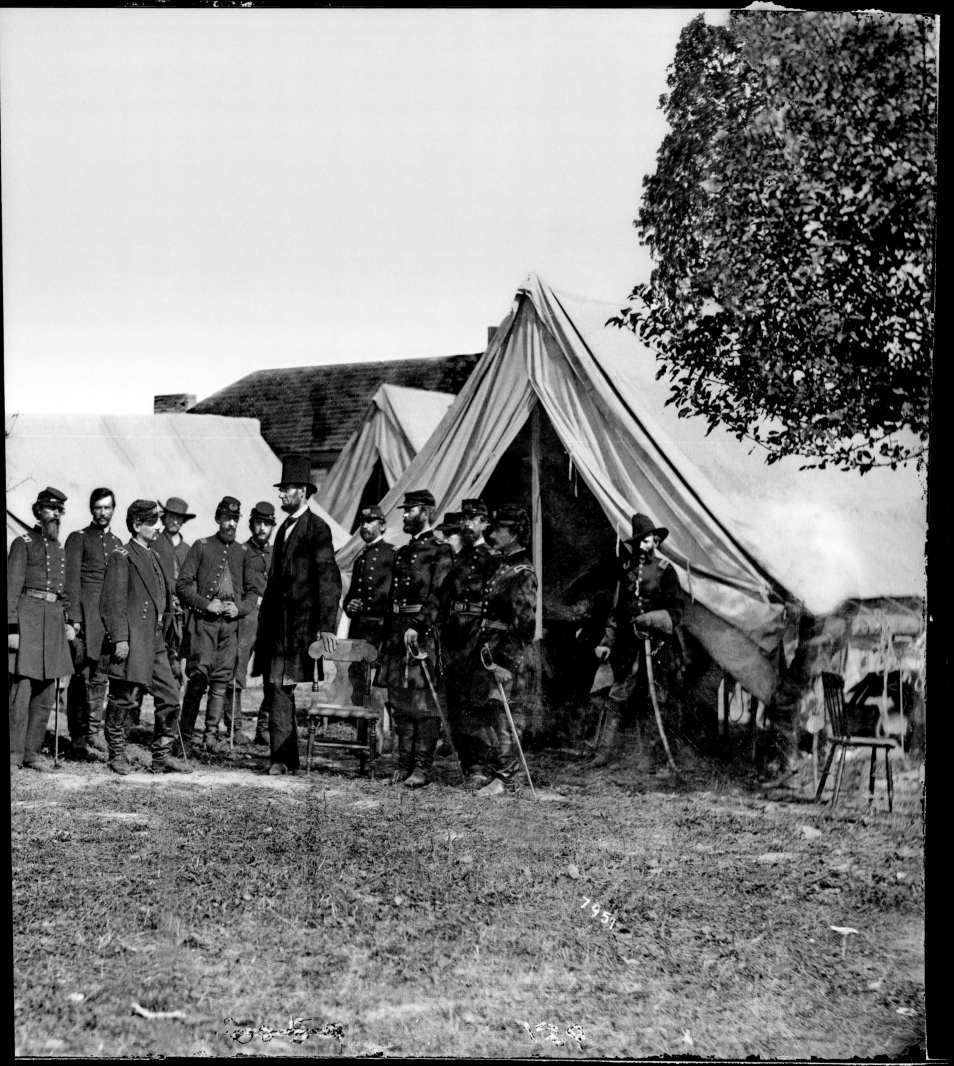

On Thursday, November 19, 1863, about twelve thousand people gathered in Gettysburg, Pennsylvania, to commemorate the Battle of Gettysburg, which had occurred there the preceding July. They were also marking the establishment of a new national soldiers' cemetery to reinter the victims from hastily prepared field graves following the battle. President Abraham Lincoln delivered a speech to dedicate the ground as a national shrine and, although he spoke for little more than two minutes, his "Gettysburg Address" was to become remembered as one of the greatest orations in American history. This image, taken by David Bachrach when he was eighteen years old, is the only confirmed photograph of Lincoln on that day. Bachrach went on to become an important photographer and the founder of Bachrach Photography, which still operates studios in a number of eastern U.S. cities. This photograph was identified in the Mathew Brady collection of photographic plates in the National Archives and Records Administration in 1952. *(November 19, 1863. David Bachrach, photographer.)*

☛ A closer view of Abraham Lincoln in Gettysburg on the day he delivered his Gettysburg Address. Seated to Lincoln's right is his bodyguard, Ward Hill Lamon.

7
CASUALTIES

" From these honored dead we take increased devotion
to that cause for which they gave the last full measure of devotion—
that we here highly resolve that these dead shall not have died in vain—
that this nation, under God, shall have a new birth of freedom—
and that government of the people, by the people, for the people,
shall not perish from the earth. **"**

Abraham Lincoln

For the first time, Civil War–era photographers were able to show the terrible and gruesome reality of war to the general American public. The impact of their work is difficult for us to now comprehend, yet in the mid-1800s nothing like it had ever been seen before in the United States (the Crimean War had been documented in Europe, but to a far lesser degree). The photographers were quite aware of the intensity and impact of their pictures. In fact, for the purpose of making a stronger statement and creating a more dynamic image, it became quite common for them to move bodies and weapons around, thereby capturing a better picture.

In 1862, Mathew Brady shocked America by displaying photographs of dead soldiers from the Antietam battlefield at his New York gallery. That exhibition marked the first time that most Northerners were actually able to see the devastating reality and carnage of war. The *New York Times* wrote that Brady had brought "home to us the terrible reality and earnestness of war."

Alexander Gardner, another well-known Civil War photographer, published the first volume of *Gardner's Photographic Sketch Book of the War* in 1865. That book included the striking photograph "The Harvest of Death" made by Timothy H. O'Sullivan, which shows bodies strewn across a field following the Battle of Gettysburg.

The appalling death toll from the Civil War is greater than the total number of fatalities from all other wars in which the United States has fought—620,000: 360,000 Northerners and 260,000 Southerners. Of these numbers, approximately 110,000 Union and 94,000 Confederate men died from wounds received directly in battle. While most soldiers feared bullets and shelling as the greatest danger, disease was actually the larger scourge. Twice as many men died from disease as from gunshot wounds: of the Federal dead, roughly three out of five; of the Confederate dead, around two out of three are believed to have perished from disease.

The most common small-arms ammunition was the minié ball, which created an enormous wound on impact. Because of the bullet's large size, a head or abdominal wound was almost always fatal, and it shattered virtually any bone it impacted. If a minié ball was capable of this sort of damage, consider the devastating carnage that resulted from antipersonnel artillery shells.

Of the estimated 175,000 wounded limbs of Federal troops, about 30,000 required amputation. It is assumed that roughly the same proportion occurred in the Confederate army. Lieutenant Colonel William W. Blackford, in his memoir *War Years with Jeb Stuart*, described the scene inside a surgeon's tent: "Tables about breast high had been erected upon which the screaming victims were having legs and arms cut off. The surgeons and their assistants, stripped to the waist and bespattered with blood, stood around, some holding the poor fellows while others, armed with long, bloody knives and saws, cut and sawed away with frightful rapidity, throwing the mangled limbs on a pile nearby as soon as removed."

Victims who survived their battlefield wounds or amputations then faced an even greater danger from infection. William Hammond, the surgeon general of the Union army stated that the Civil War occurred "at the end of the medical Middle Ages." Medical conditions were indeed appalling and primitive. Doctors did not yet completely understand that cleanliness mitigated infections, and the horrid conditions of the battlefield made frequent cleaning of their work areas and instruments difficult or impossible. "Surgical fevers"—as the subsequent infections were called—as well as gangrene became quite common following surgery.

In addition to post-surgical infections, about half of disease-related deaths during the Civil War were due to intestinal disorders: dysentery, diarrhea, and typhoid fever. These were a direct result of the utter filth found in army camps, which were "littered with refuse, food and other rubbish, sometimes in an offensive state of decomposition; slops deposited in pits within the camp limits or thrown out broadcast; heaps of manure and offal close to the camp," according to a report by the U.S. Sanitary Commission in 1864. Bowel disorders were universally widespread, as typically more than nine hundred out of every one thousand men contracted chronic diarrhea or dysentery at one time or another. Typhoid fever, caused by consuming contaminated food or water, was equally as devastating, as was malaria, which struck about a quarter of all Civil War soldiers during the war.

As the war progressed, the medical situation on both sides improved. At the start of the war in 1861, the Union army had a mere 98 medical officers and the Confederacy only 24. By 1865, around 13,000 Union and 4,000 Confederate medical officers and doctors had served at battlefields and hospitals. The overwhelming and dire needs of the Civil War ultimately gave birth to the rise of improved medical treatment, superior conditions of cleanliness, better medical records, and more surgeons becoming knowledgeable in the use of anesthetics. The universal appreciation and respect from patients and doctors alike ☛

of the work performed by female nurses gave rise to a new and growing medical field for women.

During the early years of the war, a new profession emerged—the "embalming surgeon." In 1861, Dr. Thomas Holmes of New York, known as the "father of modern embalming" had developed a process to preserve a dead body for an extended period of time. He drained blood from the body and then pumped an arsenic-based fluid into the veins, which prevented decay. As more and more soldiers were killed in battle, many families wanted their loved ones' bodies returned home. Although expensive, this new embalming process made it possible to ship bodies home for burial.

An embalming surgeon would set up his operation in an available shed, building, or tent near a hospital or battlefield and ply his trade. At times there might be dozens or even a hundred or more bodies waiting to be embalmed. Later in the war, as the process gained wider acceptance, it became commonplace for the remains of the majority of identified soldiers to be embalmed and shipped back home.

With all the hazards both on the battlefield and in the camps, a Civil War soldier's chance of not surviving the war was about one in four. Wounded men were cared for by an underqualified, understaffed, and undersupplied medical corps working against incredible odds. ❖

Dead Confederate soldiers (opposite) lie in a ditch that had been used as a rifle pit during the Battle of Antietam in Maryland; Union soldiers congregate on the edge (below, detail). That battle, on September 17, 1862, was General Lee's first attempt to bring the war into Northern territory. The battle was inconclusive, although it did drive Lee's forces out of Maryland. (*September 1862. Alexander Gardner, photographer.*)

Confederate dead at the edge of Rose's Woods after the Battle of Gettysburg. Although the single-day death toll was greater at the Battle of Antietam almost a year earlier, the Battle of Gettysburg, which spanned three days (July 1 to 3, 1863), was responsible for an estimated fifty-one thousand casualties. More men fought and died there than in any other battle on North American soil. *(July 5, 1863. Alexander Gardner, photographer.)*

Confederate dead gathered for burial at the southwestern edge of Rose's Woods, after the Battle of Gettysburg. Lee's retreat began on the afternoon of Saturday, July 4, 1863. He was forced to abandon his dead as Confederate wounded were loaded onto wagons and the Southern army staggered back from the battlefield, physically and spiritually exhausted. Although the war continued for another two years, the Confederacy never recovered from their losses at Gettysburg. *(July 5, 1863. Timothy O'Sullivan, photographer.)*

A dead Confederate soldier in the Devil's Den at Gettysburg, Pennsylvania. "Devil's Den" is a name given to an outcropping of massive boulders that was the site of fierce fighting on July 2, 1863, the second day of the Battle of Gettysburg. *(July 1863. Alexander Gardner, photographer.)*

Bodies of Federal soldiers killed on July 1, 1863, near McPherson Woods at Gettysburg, Pennsylvania. The Battle of Gettysburg was General Lee's second and final attempt to bring the war into the North. With about 88,000 Union troops pitted against 70,000 Confederate troops, Gettysburg was one of the fiercest battles of the war. Although costly to both sides, the North emerged victorious, and historians often describe this battle as the turning point of the Civil War. *(July 1863. Timothy O'Sullivan, photographer.)*

Four dead soldiers in the woods near Little Round Top
in Gettysburg, Pennsylvania. "Little Round Top" is the
smaller of two rocky hills that were the site of an unsuccessful
assault by Confederate troops against the Union left flank
on July 2, 1863, the second day of the Battle of Gettysburg.
(*July 1863. Alexander Gardner, photographer.*)

Another dead Confederate soldier in the Devil's Den, killed on July 2, 1863, the second day of fighting in the Battle of Gettysburg. *(July 1863. Alexander Gardner, photographer.)*

The burial of Federal dead at Fredericksburg, Virginia. The Battle of the Wilderness was fought on May 5 and 6, 1864, in an area of rough terrain and dense scrub growth in Spotsylvania and Orange counties, Virginia. This was the first battle of General Grant's Overland Campaign against General Lee. Both armies suffered heavy casualties, though the battle was inconclusive. The caption on the sleeve of this negative reads: "Burial scene under flag of truce, May 12, 1864." (*1864. Probably Timothy O'Sullivan, photographer.*)

☞ A closer detail of Federal soldiers burying their dead at Fredericksburg, Virginia.

The body of a Confederate soldier at the home of widow Susan Alsop near Spotsylvania Court House, Virginia, a casualty of the Battle of Spotsylvania. Fought from May 8 to 21, it was the second major battle in General Grant's 1864 Wilderness Campaign, and pitted 56,000 Confederate soldiers against a Union army numbering 101,000 men. This is one of the most compelling photographs of Confederate dead taken at Mrs. Alsop's farm on May 20, 1864. Uncontestable records affirm the soldier to be a Confederate, yet he is clearly wearing a Union belt, which is upside down. Does the fact it is inverted signify it was taken from a dead Northern soldier, or was it merely a souvenir of war? *(May 20, 1864. Timothy O'Sullivan, photographer.)*

The body of another Confederate soldier at Mrs. Alsop's house near Spotsylvania Courthouse, Virginia. The title "Mrs." Alsop suggests an elderly matron, but in fact, Susan Alsop was only twenty-three years old in 1864. Her husband, James Alsop, had died in December of 1860 before the war. Mrs. Alsop never remarried, never moved away, and lived out her remaining half-century of life on the farm where these pictures were taken. *(May 20, 1864. Timothy O'Sullivan, photographer.)*

Dr. Bunnell's field embalming station for the Army of the James. Typical of Civil War embalming operations, this is one of Dr. Bunnell's embalming sheds near Fredericksburg, Virginia. *(December 1862. Photographer unknown.)*

Dr. Richard Burr, an embalming surgeon, seen processing a soldier's body recovered from an unknown battlefield. *(Date and photographer unknown.)*

A dead Confederate soldier with a gun at Petersburg, Virginia. This haunting and well-known photograph clearly brings home the devastating finality of battle. Note how the photographer has carefully positioned the guns in relation to the soldier's body, a technique many Civil War photographers used to achieve a more powerful image. *(April 3, 1865. Photographer unknown.)*

Confederate and Union dead side-by-side in the trenches at Fort Mahone. The third Battle of Petersburg, also known as the Breakthrough at Petersburg, was a decisive Union assault on the Confederate trenches that ended the ten-month siege. This victory led to the fall of Richmond, and ultimately the end of the war. *(April 3, 1865. Photographer unknown.)*

Soldiers' Cemetery at Alexandria, Virginia.
While neither as large nor as famous as its nearby
neighbor in Arlington, Alexandria National
Cemetery, as it is formally called, was established by
the Union army in 1862. Of the more than 3,500
Union soldiers buried here, more than 220 are
African Americans. *(Date and photographer unknown.)*

☞ A closer view of maintenance personnel
at the Alexandria National Cemetery.

8

CONCLUSION

" With malice toward none; with charity for all;

with firmness in the right, as God gives us to see the right,

let us strive on to finish the work we are in; to bind up the nation's wounds;

to care for him who shall have borne the battle,

and for his widow and his orphan — to do all which may achieve and cherish a just,

and a lasting peace, among ourselves, and with all nations. "

Abraham Lincoln

In April 1865, following four years of conflict, the terrible war came to an end.

After fleeing Richmond, Virginia, on April 2, 1865, following Grant's victory there, General Lee's exhausted Confederate army arrived in the county seat of Amelia Court House two days later. The goal was to resupply the army there, but no provisions could be found. Lee's army, which by then numbered no more than 9,000 cavalry and infantry troops, headed west to Appomattox Station, where supply trains still awaited him. On April 8, 1Union cavalry under the command of Brigadier General George Armstrong Custer arrived at the town of Appomattox Station first. They captured and burned the three supply trains that had been waiting there for Lee's army.

With his supplies at Appomattox destroyed, Lee then looked west to Lynchburg, Virginia, where more supplies awaited at the railway there. Although the Union army was closing in, all that lay between Lee and Lynchburg was Union cavalry. Lee hoped to break through the cavalry before Union infantry reinforcements arrived, but it was not to be.

At dawn on Sunday, April 9, 1865, the Confederates attacked General Sheridan's cavalry. They charged through the Union lines and took the ridge, but as they reached the crest they saw the entire Union line of battle in front of them, forcing Lee to finally state the inevitable, "There is nothing left for me to do but to go and see General Grant, and I would rather die a thousand deaths."

The home of grocer Wilmer McLean in the nearby village of Appomattox Court House was chosen as the most appropriate place to hold the meeting between generals Grant and Lee. Ironically, McLean had lived near Manassas Junction during the First Battle of Bull Run in 1861, and moved to Appomattox to escape the war.

Dressed in an immaculate uniform with a fine sword, Lee waited for Grant to arrive. Grant entered unarmed, in a mud-spattered privates' uniform, with only the stars on his tarnished shoulder straps to show his rank. It was the first time the two men had seen each other face-to-face in almost two decades since they had both served in the Mexican-American War.

Grant's terms of surrender were as charitable and gracious as possible. He confiscated the arms from Lee's men, agreed that they would not be charged with treason or imprisoned, and allowed the defeated soldiers to keep their horses and mules to carry out spring planting. Grant also supplied Lee with food and water for his famished army, which Lee said, "would have a very happy effect among the men and do much toward reconciling the country." Around four o'clock on Sunday, April 9, 1865, the terms of surrender were signed. The Federal troops starting cheering as Lee left the house and rode away, but Grant quickly put an end to that, reasoning, "The Confederates were now our countrymen and we did not want to exult over their downfall." The formal ceremony of surrender occurred on April 12, 1865—four years to the day from the attack on Fort Sumter that began the war.

On April 14, 1865—Good Friday and the day of the flag-raising ceremony at Fort Sumter—at approximately 10:15 PM, Abraham Lincoln was assassinated at Ford's Theater in Washington, D.C. For most of the country the tragedy of Lincoln's death—he was the first U.S. president to be assassinated—overshadowed the joy brought about by the end of hostilities.

The Sunday following Lincoln's death, Easter Sunday, millions of Americans attended memorial services in Washington and around the country. On Tuesday, April 18,

President Lincoln's body lay in state in the East Room of the White House. About 25,000 citizens filed past the coffin, which was placed on a platform draped in black cloth in the darkened room. A silver plate on the lid of the coffin read simply: "Abraham Lincoln, 16th President of the United States, Born February 12, 1809, Died April 15, 1865."

The funeral itself was held shortly after noon on the next day. Following the brief service, a funeral hearse drawn by six white horses took the coffin on a three-mile-long procession past an estimated 100,000 citizens lining the streets to the Capitol Building. Lincoln's body then lay in state in the newly finished Capitol rotunda the following day, where thousands more paid their respects.

On Friday, April 21, President Abraham Lincoln left Washington for the last time. A funeral train called the "Lincoln Special" retraced the route that had first brought him to Washington following his election to the presidency in 1861. During the thirteen-day, 1,700-mile trip, accounts suggest that about 12 million people saw the train en route as it returned Lincoln to his home in Springfield, Illinois. On May 4, 1865, Lincoln's body was placed in its tomb.

The war may have been over, but its costs lingered on. The United States government estimated in January of 1863, halfway through the war, that it was then costing 2.5 million dollars each day—a huge sum in those days. A final official estimate compiled in 1879 put the total cost at 6.2 billion dollars for the North; the Confederacy spent about 2.1 billion dollars. Shortly after the turn of the century, another 3.3 billion dollars already had been spent by the U.S. government on pensions and other benefits for former Federal soldiers. Southern states provided benefits to Confederate veterans as well. Eventually, the amount spent on benefits far exceeded the war's original cost.

In addition to the direct monetary cost, the physical devastation was enormous. The wreckage of burned homes, lost crops and livestock, ruined buildings and bridges, and ravaged cities left the South in utter ruin.

Beyond all of that, though, was the overwhelming loss of lives—620,000 husbands, brothers, and sons dead. ❖

The crowd inside Fort Sumter awaiting the flag-raising ceremony at Charleston, South Carolina. Major Robert Anderson was in command of Fort Sumter when it was bombarded by the Confederates, beginning the Civil War, on April 12, 1861. Badly outnumbered and outgunned, he was forced to surrender on April 14, even though no one on either side was killed in the battle. As his troops evacuated Sumter, Anderson took the flag that had flown over the fort with him. During the war, repeated attempts by Union forces to take Charleston or batter its defenses proved futile as Confederate defenses held firm. In 1863, the Union began a major offensive campaign against the defenses of Charleston Harbor. Later, as General Sherman marched through South Carolina, the situation for Charleston became ever more precarious. Finally, on February 15, 1865, Confederate forces were ordered to evacuate. When news of the evacuation reached Washington, President Lincoln proposed a celebration to mark the event. Mere days after Lee's surrender at Appomattox, Anderson returned to Fort Sumter for the celebration. Four years to the day after lowering the flag in surrender, he raised it in triumph over the recaptured but badly damaged fort. *(April 14, 1865. Jacob Coonley, photographer.)*

The McLean house at Appomattox Court House, Virginia, was originally built in 1848 as a tavern. Wilmer McLean bought the house in 1863 for use as a private residence. A retired major in the Virginia militia, McLean had been too old to enlist at the outbreak of the Civil War. After one of the initial battles of the war, the First Battle of Bull Run, took place in part on his farm near Manassas, Virginia, McLean sought to avoid the war by buying this house and moving to Appomattox Court House. Nonetheless, in April of 1865, the war came back to McLean, when General Robert E. Lee surrendered to General Ulysses S. Grant at McLean's house. Later, McLean would boast that the Civil War began in his backyard and ended in his parlor. (April 1865. Timothy O'Sullivan, photographer.)

Following his surrender, the beloved Confederate general Robert E. Lee faced as uncertain a future as his defeated troops. He traveled the ninety miles from Appomattox to Richmond and set up residence at 707 East Franklin Street in a house that his son Custis had rented. Upon entering his new home, he is said to have declared that it was the last time he would ever wear a sword. His fame was such that Union soldiers were stationed there to protect Lee from crowds of adoring well-wishers who sought him out. On April 16, 1865, mere days after the surrender, Mathew Brady made this famous photograph of General Lee as he stood on the front porch of the Richmond house. The photo appears to have been touched up by hand somewhere in its history. *(April 16, 1865. Mathew Brady, photographer.)*

No 762

Ford's Theatre in Washington, D.C., with guards posted at the entrances and mourning crepe draped from the windows. Just five days after General Lee's surrender, President Lincoln and his wife attended a performance at Ford's Theatre. John Wilkes Booth, a famous actor, desperate to aid the dying Confederacy, stepped into the box where the presidential party was sitting and shot Lincoln. The president died the next morning. Following the assassination, the U.S. Government appropriated the theater, paying 100,000 dollars in compensation, and issued an order forever prohibiting its use as a place of public amusement. *(April 1865. Photographer unknown.)*

☞ A closer view detailing some of the citizens milling about in front of Ford's Theatre on 10th Street N.W. in Washington, D.C. Notice the man reading a newspaper in his room on the second floor of the building next door to the theater.

President Lincoln's box at Ford's Theatre. Lincoln's box seat had been specially decorated for the presidential party during the afternoon before the assassination. Four American flags and a Treasury Department regimental flag were set in place, George Washington's engraving was put in the middle, and special furniture was moved in. An upholstered rocker was placed at the far right corner for Lincoln so that he would be hidden from the audience's view. *(April 1865. Photographer unknown.)*

President Abraham Lincoln's funeral procession on Pennsylvania Avenue in Washington, D.C., April 19, 1865. Following the funeral ceremony held in the Green Room at the White House, twelve army sergeants carried the coffin to a hearse pulled by six white horses. The procession slowly took the slain president to the newly constructed Capitol Building where his body would lay in state the following day, viewed by 25,000 people. The crowd that viewed the procession itself was estimated at 100,000 citizens, described by *Frank Leslie's Illustrated Newspaper*: "Every window, housetop, balcony and every inch of the sidewalks on either side was densely crowded with a mournful throng. . . . Despite the enormous crowd the silence was profound. It seemed akin to the death it commemorated. . . . A solemn sadness reigned everywhere. . . . The monotonous thump of the funeral drum sounded in the street." *(April 19, 1865. Photographer unknown.)*

After the memorials in Washington, D.C., Lincoln's body was taken by train to his hometown of Springfield, Illinois. "The Lincoln Special," as the funeral train was called, passed through 444 communities in seven states and was viewed by millions. At virtually every stop, remembrances were held for the late president, making it "The Greatest Funeral in the History of the United States." On Thursday, May 3, 1865, the train finally arrived at Springfield. One final remembrance was held, and the next day, Abraham Lincoln, sixteenth president of the United States, was laid to rest. The ornate hearse seen here was borrowed from the city of Saint Louis to carry the president's body on the final leg of his final journey. *(1865. S.M. Fassett, photographer.)*

Captain Nevins and officers posing in front of their headquarters at Fort Whipple in Arlington, Virginia. This photo was taken a full two months after the assassination, and the black crepe displayed over the door and windows indicates that the country was still in a state of grief and mourning for the slain president. (June 1865. William Morris Smith, photographer.)

☛ A closer view of Captain Nevins and his officers at Fort Whipple. The fort was named for Major General Amiel Weeks Whipple, who died at the Battle of Chancellorsville. Situated immediately across the Potomac River in Arlington, the fort was one of the strongest fortifications built to defend Washington, D.C.

The Grand Review of the Armies, Washington, D.C., showing some of the thousands of infantry marching in the parade as they passed along Pennsylvania Avenue near the Treasury, with the new Capitol building in the distance. The two-day parade and celebration was unlike anything the nation's capital had ever seen. *(May 23 or 24, 1865. Mathew Brady, photographer.)*

EPILOGUE

In May 1865, as a declaration that the rebellion and armed resistance was finally at an end, the nation threw the biggest parade it had ever seen, almost as proof that the Union still stood. They called it the Grand Review of the Armies, and hundreds of regiments and thousands of soldiers marched through Washington in sight of the newly erected Capitol building. On a bright and sunny Tuesday morning on May 23, Major General George Meade, the victor of Gettysburg, marched an estimated eighty thousand men in sharp military precision past crowds that numbered into the thousands. The infantry marched twelve men across, followed by the artillery corps, and then an array of cavalry regiments that stretched for another seven miles. The mood was one of gaiety and celebration, decidedly different from the feeling of gloom and mourning that had descended over the capital following the assassination of President Lincoln barely a month before.

On the following morning, General William Tecumseh Sherman led sixty-five thousand men from the Army of the Tennessee and the Army of Georgia along the same route. For six hours, under bright sunshine, the men who had marched through Georgia now paraded in front of the joyous throngs that lined the sidewalks and peered from windows and rooftops. Unlike Meade's troops, Sherman's more ragtag army was followed by civilians who had traveled with his forces north from Savannah: freed slaves, farmers, fortune hunters, and other opportunists. There was even a herd of confiscated cattle, goats, and pack mules.

When it was over, most soldiers simply went home. The war had been the defining point of their generation and, to varying degrees, it had changed them all. But, the men returned home to their families and loved ones and went about resuming their lives as much as possible.

Ulysses S. Grant, the general-in-chief of the Union army, went on to become the eighteenth president of the United States, from 1869 to 1877. His administration was marred by scandal and, after being left destitute by a fraudulent investor following his presidency, Grant wrote his memoirs. In 1884, Grant, who had been suffering from cancer, died several days after completing his writing. He was sixty-three years old.

After the surrender, Robert E. Lee returned to Richmond, assumed the presidency of Washington College (now Washington and Lee University) in Lexington, Virginia, and died on October 12, 1870, following a stroke. He, along with other Confederates, had been pardoned for treason by President Andrew Johnson in a proclamation dated Christmas Day, 1868. Lee was officially reinstated as a U.S. citizen by President Gerald Ford in 1975.

William Tecumseh Sherman was put in charge of the Military Division of Missouri just three months after Lee's surrender. His duties were to protect the progress of railroad construction from attack by Native Americans. When Grant became president, Sherman was appointed commanding general of the U.S. Army. He published his memoirs in 1875 and retired from the army in 1884. When he was suggested as a Republican candidate for president in 1884, he quashed the proposition by stating, "I will not accept if nominated and will not serve if elected." Sherman died in New York City on February 14, 1891. His body was transported to St. Louis, where the burial was presided over by his son, Thomas Ewing Sherman, a Jesuit priest.

Confederate general Joseph E. Johnston moved to Richmond, Virginia, after the war and served as a Democratic congressman from 1879 to 1881. When Sherman died, Johnston acted as an honorary pallbearer at the New York City procession on February 19, 1891. It was a bitterly cold day and a friend of Johnston, fearing for the old general's health, asked him to put on his hat. Out of respect, Johnston refused. "If I were in [Sherman's] place, and he were standing in mine, he would not put on his hat." Johnston caught pneumonia and died several weeks later.

Jefferson Davis, president of the Confederate States of America for its entire history from 1861 to 1865, was charged with treason following his capture in May of 1865. He was jailed at Fort Monroe on the Virginia coast, and after two years of imprisonment, he was released on a bail of 100 thousand dollars. Although he was never tried, he was, however, declared ineligible to run for any public office. On December 2, 1889, he died in New Orleans at eighty-one years of age. In 1978, President Jimmy Carter posthumously restored to Davis his U.S. citizenship.

Over time, the remaining North and South combatants faded away. The last living documented veteran of the Civil War was Albert Woolson, a Union drummer boy from Minnesota, who died in 1956 at age 109. All that now remains of the war are memories, monuments, memorials . . . and old photographs. ❖

ACKNOWLEDGMENTS

First and foremost I wish to thank my wonderful wife Dixie Foust for her continued suggestions, support, and, especially, her unflagging belief in this project and in me. My brother Dan Guntzelman and his wife Lissa Levin were equally supportive and a great help, critiquing early drafts of text and offering thoughtful suggestions. Unlimited thanks to my agent Kathy Green and to Barbara Berger, executive editor at Sterling Publications, for their strong belief in this book and their assistance in getting it before the public. I am especially grateful to assistant editor Sasha Tropp and to Barbara, for their elegant polishing of my text, and also to designers Perri DeFino and Susan Welt of *gonzalez defino editorial & design* for the book's beautiful layout and design. Without them, my dream would never have become reality. I am also most indebted to Bob Zeller, president of The Center for Civil War Photography and a leading authority on Civil War imagery, for his eloquent and knowledgeable foreword to this book.

As always, I am grateful to my son Kris for his computer savvy and website skills, which bailed me out on a number of occasions, especially after one devastating hard drive crash. Over the duration of creating a project such as this, many people have assisted me to a greater or lesser degree; some directly by their knowledge and contacts, some indirectly by their friendship or merely a positive word. I would be remiss if I did not mention their names and offer them public thanks. Many thanks, then, to Paul Wilson, Craig Clyde, David L. Smith, Michael Breeding, Ken Williamson, Sam Stephens, Molly Maguire, Aaron Silverman, Bruce Vinokour, and Marsha Cook. Finally, I am especially grateful to the many dedicated yet unheralded technicians at the Library of Congress. Without their diligent and meticulous work scanning and preserving these remarkable historic photos, *The Civil War in Color* would never have been possible. ❖

REFERENCES

Books

Basler, Roy P., Marion Dolores Pratt, and Lloyd A. Dunlap, eds. *The Collected Works of Abraham Lincoln*, 8 vols. Piscataway, NJ: Rutgers University Press, 1953–55. http://quod.lib.umich.edu/l/lincoln/

Blackford, William W. *War Years with Jeb Stuart*. New York: Scribner, 1945.

Boyd, James Penny. *Military and Civil Life of Gen. Ulysses S. Grant*. Philadelphia: Garreston & Co., 1885.

"Brady's Photographs: Pictures of the Dead at Antietam." *New York Times*, October 20, 1862. http://www.nytimes.com/1862/10/20/news/brady-s-photographs-pictures-of-the-dead-at-antietam.html?pagewanted=all

Documents of the U.S. Sanitary Commission, vol. 1. New York: United States Sanitary Commission, 1866. http://books.google.com/books/reader?id=bIwAAAAYAAJ&printsec=frontcover&output=reader

Gardner, Alexander. *Gardner's Photographic Sketchbook of the Civil War*. New York: Dover, 1959.

Garrison, Webb. *Civil War Curiosities: Strange Stories, Oddities, Events, and Coincidences*. Nashville, TN: Rutledge Hill, 1995.

Holland, Frederic May. *Frederick Douglass: The Colored Orator*. New York: Funk & Wagnalls, 1891.

Kagan, Neil, and Stephen G. Hyslop. *Eyewitness to the Civil War: The Complete History from Secession to Reconstruction*. Washington, DC: National Geographic, 2006.

Lee, Robert Edward. *Recollections and Letters of General Robert E. Lee*. New York: Doubleday, 1904. http://books.google.com/books?id=SzkDAAAAYAAJ&printsec=frontcover&dq=Lee,+Robert+Edward&hl=en&sa=X&ei=NTiHT63sMsi0gwfchtThBw&ved=0CDgQ6AEwAA#v=onepage&q=Lee%2C%20Robert%20Edward&f=false

Miller, Francis Trevelyan, and Robert S. Lanier, eds. *The Photographic History of the Civil War in Ten Volumes*. 10 vols. New York: The Review of Reviews, 1911. http://www.scribd.com/collections/2622146/The-Photographic-History-of-the-Civil-War-in-Ten-Volumes-1911

Nevins, Allan. *The War for the Union: The Improvised War, 1861–1862*, vol. 1. New York: Scribner, 1950.

Oates, Steven B. *Abraham Lincoln: The Man Behind the Myths*. New York: HarperCollins, 1984.

Sherman, William Tecumseh. *General Sherman's Official Account of His Great March Through Georgia and . . .* New York: Bunce & Huntington, 1865.

Symonds, Craig L. *Joseph E. Johnston: A Civil War Biography*. New York: W. W. Norton, 1992.

Wilson, Rufus Rockwell, ed. *Lincoln Among His Friends: A Sheaf of Intimate Memories*. Caldwell, ID: Caxton, 1942.

Winik, Jay, *April 1865: The Month That Saved America*. New York: HarperCollins, 2001.

Websites

AmericanCivilWar.com "Appomattox Court House Virginia," http://americancivilwar.com/appo.html

"Ulysses S. Grant: Union Civil War General," http://americancivilwar.com/north/grant.html

"Union Navy Ship USS *Monitor*," http://americancivilwar.com/monitor.html

CivilWarWiki.Net "Dictator Mortar," http://civilwarwiki.net/wiki/The_Dictator_Mortar

"12 pdr. 'Napoleon' Light Field Gun," http://civilwarwiki.net/wiki/12_pdr._%22Napoleon%22_Light_Field_Gun

Library of Congress *American Memory*, "Contrabands of War," http://memory.loc.gov/ammem/aaohtml/exhibit/aopart4.html

American Memory, "Selected Civil War Photographs," http://memory.loc.gov/ammem/cwphtml/cwphome.html

National Park Service *Civil War Series*, "The Civil War's Common Soldier," http://www.nps.gov/history/history/online_books/civil_war_series/3/sec2.htm

"Harpers Ferry Armory and Arsenal," http://www.nps.gov/hafe/historyculture/harpers-ferry-armory-and-arsenal.htm

National Records and Archives Administration *American Originals*, "Civil War and Reconstruction," http://www.archives.gov/exhibits/american_originals/civilwar.html

Teachers, "Teaching With Documents: The Fight for Equal Rights: Black Soldiers in the Civil War," http://www.archives.gov/education/lessons/blacks-civil-war/

Shotgun's Home of the American Civil War "Civil War Nurses: 'The Angels of the Battlefield,'" http://www.civilwarhome.com/civilwarnurses.htm

"Cost of the American Civil War," http://www.civilwarhome.com/warcosts.htm

"Jefferson Davis," http://www.civilwarhome.com/jdavisbio.htm

"Joseph Eggleston Johnston," http://www.civilwarhome.com/joejohnston.htm

"Medical Care, Battle Wounds, and Disease," http://www.civilwarhome.com/civilwarmedicine.htm

"The Price in Blood!: Casualties in the Civil War," http://www.civilwarhome.com/casualties.htm

"The Sanitary Commission and Other Relief Agencies," http://www.civilwarhome.com/sanitary-commission.htm

"Slavery in the Civil War Era," http://www.civilwarhome.com/slavery.htm

"Weapons of the American Civil War," http://www.civilwarhome.com/weapons.htm

Wikipedia http://en.wikipedia.org/wiki/Assassination_of_Abraham_Lincoln - cite_note-77#cite_note-77

http://en.wikipedia.org/wiki/Battle_of_Appomattox_Station

http://en.wikipedia.org/wiki/Carte_de_visite

http://en.wikipedia.org/wiki/Charleston,_South_Carolina_in_the_American_Civil_War

http://en.wikipedia.org/wiki/Dahlgren_gun

http://en.wikipedia.org/wiki/Harpers_Ferry,_West_Virginia

http://en.wikipedia.org/wiki/Parrott_rifle

http://en.wikipedia.org/wiki/Richmond_in_the_American_Civil_War

http://en.wikipedia.org/wiki/Slavery_in_the_United_States

http://en.wikipedia.org/wiki/United_States_Constitution

http://en.wikipedia.org/wiki/William_Tecumseh_Sherman

http://en.wikipedia.org/wiki/Zouave#American_Zouave_uniforms

Other Sites

Alexandria Library, "Civil War Era Burials—Alexandria National Cemetery," http://www.alexandria.lib.va.us/lhsc_genealogy_resources/alex_natl_cem/cem.html

American Civil War Photo Gallery, http://www.civilwarpictures.com/history-of-civilwar-photography.html

CaptainBlakely.org, "Cannon for the South," http://captainblakely.org/CannonfortheSouth.aspx

Center for Civil War Photography, http://www.civilwarphotography.org

Cincinnati Civil War Round Table, "Lincoln at the Civil War Battlefields," http://www.cincinnaticwrt.org/data/Summaries_recent%20talks/Billings_Lincoln%20at%20the%20Civil%20War%20Battlefields.html

City of Alexandria, Virginia, "Contrabands and Freedmen's Cemetery Memorial, Design Competition 2008," http://www3.alexandriava.gov/freedmens/pdf/HistoricReferences.pdf

CivilWarAcademy.com, "Civil War Food," http://www.civilwaracademy.com/civil-war-food.html

Civil War Artillery Projectiles, Jack W. Melton Jr., http://www.civilwarartillery.com/

Civil War Crossroads, Harpers Ferry, http://www.civilwarsites.com/html/harpersferry.asp

Civil War Voices Soldier Studies, "American Civil War Soldier WebQuest," http://www.soldierstudies.org/index.php?action=webquest_1

Cleveland Civil War Roundtable, "Lincoln and the Black Hawk War," Dale Thomas, http://clevelandcivilwarroundtable.com/articles/lincoln/blackhawk_war.htm

Economic History Association, "Slavery in the United States," Jenny B. Wahl, http://eh.net/encyclopedia/article/wahl.slavery.us

"Embalming Surgeons and Undertakers," http://www.civilwarundertaker.net/history.htm

Georgia's Blue and Gray Trail, "Surrender at Appomattox," http://blueandgraytrail.com/event/Surrender_At_Appomattox

GreatAmericanHistory.net, "Religious Revival in Civil War Armies," Gordon Leidner, http://www.greatamericanhistory.net/revival.htm

History.com, "10 Surprising Civil War Facts," http://www.history.com/news/2011/05/10/10-surprising-civil-war-facts/

Iowa State University Center for Agricultural History and Rural Studies, American Agricultural History Primer, "The Cotton Economy of the Old South," http://www.history.iastate.edu/agprimer/Page28.html

Learning-Online, "The Telegraph in the War Room," Howard Taylor, http://www.alincoln-learning.us/Civilwartelegraphing.html

"Lincoln's Funeral," http://www.angelfire.com/my/abraham-lincoln/Funeral.html

Metropolitan Museum of Art, Heilbrunn Timeline of Art History, "Photography and the Civil War," http://www.metmuseum.org/toah/hd/phcw/hd_phcw.htm

Morrisville State College Library, "Albert Woolson," http://localhistory.morrisville.edu/sites/gar_post/woolson.html

Mr. Lincoln and Friends, a project of the Lincoln Institute. "Horace White (1834-1916)," http://www.mrlincolnandfriends.org/inside.asp?pageID=114&subjectID=44th paragraph

MrLincolnsWhiteHouse.org, "President Lincoln's Funeral," http://www.mrlincolnswhitehouse.org/inside.asp?ID=213&subjectID=2

NetPlaces.com, American Civil War, "Life in the Service: Uniforms," http://www.netplaces.com/american-civil-war/life-in-the-service/uniforms.htm

NNDB.com, "Robert E. Lee," http://www.nndb.com/people/930/000049783/

Suite101.com, "The Fall of Richmond 1865," Michael Streich, http://www.suite101.com/content/the-fall-of-richmond-april-1865-a116297

United States Census Bureau, Census of Population and Housing: 1860 Census, http://www.census.gov/prod/www/abs/decennial/1860.html

USA People Search, "People of the Civil War: A Soldier's Life," http://articles.usa-people-search.com/content-people-of-the-civil-war-a-soldiers-life.aspx

U.S. Christian Commission, Northwest Branch, "History of the U.S. Christian Commission," http://www.nwuscc.org/OldUSCC.html

War for States Rights, "Artillery, Arms & Ammunition," http://civilwar.bluegrass.net/ArtilleryAndArms/dahlgrenguns.html

"Wilmer McLean: The Beginning and the End," Simon J. Pace, http://ehistory.osu.edu/world/articles/ArticleView.cfm?AID=37.asp?pageID=114&subjectID=44th paragraph

ADDITIONAL SOURCES
OF CIVIL WAR PHOTOGRAPHY

A Google search for "American Civil War" typically yields about 28 million responses! The Internet affords access to Civil War information and groups as never before, including historic sites, organizations, reenactment groups, maps, records, facts, and photographs, as well as information about armaments, generals, and battles. While researching this book, I visited literally hundreds—perhaps even a thousand or more—sites dealing with all aspects of the "War Between the States." What follows is a relatively brief list of websites dedicated to Civil War photographs.

The **U.S. Library of Congress** site is the source of the original black-and-white photographs featured in this book. The library is massive and allows downloading of digital images at various resolutions. The pictures in this book were downloaded at the highest uncompressed TIFF resolution.

http://memory.loc.gov/ammem/cwphtml/cwphome.html

The **American Civil War Photo Gallery** is a fine site organized into about twenty sections, such as infantry groups, trains and railroads, battlefields and fortifications, and artillery units.

http://www.civilwar-pictures.com/g/civil-war-pictures

The **Old Picture** website has a large collection of Civil War images, as well as a wide range of other old photographs from 1850 to 1940.

http://www.old-picture.com/civil-war-index-001.htm

Civil War Photos is another good site with a wealth of photos segregated by topic (casualties, military life, naval officers, group photos, etc.), as well as by location (Antietam, Md.; Atlanta, Ga.; Washington, D.C.; and others.)

http://www.civilwarphotos.net

Part of the American Memory collection at the Library of Congress, **Civil War Treasures from the New-York Historical Society** features drawings, letters, manuscripts, posters, and etchings, as well as photographs—including samples and descriptions of more than seven hundred original stereo cards.

http://memory.loc.gov/ammem/ndlpcoop/nhihtml/
cwnyhshome.html

The **Center for Civil War Photography** is a site where "you will find basic and complex information about Civil War photography and its practitioners." This website contains a small yet remarkable example of stereographs, in which the left and right eye images have been filtered, allowing them to be viewed on a computer monitor while wearing an inexpensive pair of red and green 3-D glasses. Although made one hundred and fifty years ago, the quality and depth of 3-D in these photos is astounding.

http://www.civilwarphotography.org

Civil War and More features photographs of African Americans during the war years. The pictures are presented as relatively high resolution JPEGs, although the collection is quite small.

http://www.negroartist.com/CIVIL%20WAR%20
AND%20MORE/

Mathew Brady Civil War Photographs is a collection from the National Archives that has been placed on the Flickr website for easy access. In addition to war-related images, the collection includes many portraits that emanated from the Brady Studios in those years. Some of these, which were made as cartes de visite, show the portrait replicated four or eight times, side-by-side.

http://www.flickr.com/photos/usnationalarchives/
collections/72157622495226723/

The **Yankee Occupation of Atlanta** website is a wonderfully detailed collection of extremely high-resolution photographs made by George Barnard from September to November 1864, during Sherman's occupation of the city. Most are labeled with names of specific streets.

http://freepages.genealogy.rootsweb.ancestry.com/~wb4kdi/
Military%20Service/Confederates/Atlanta/

Original Photographs from the Civil War is another fine website with a limited yet high-quality gallery.

http://www.mikelynaugh.com/VirtualCivilWar/New/
Originals2/index.html

INDEX

Page numbers in **boldface** indicate photographs.

PICTURE CREDITS

Collection of Bob Zeller: 8–9; 11, 12, 13

Collection of Matthew R. Isenburg: 10

Courtesy of Geography & Map Division, Library of Congress (backgrounds): 38–39: g3922c cw0155000; 56–57: g3884p cw611000; 77: gvs01 vhs00082; 88–89: gvhs01 vhs00057; 104–5: g3964n cw0432000; 119: g3912p cw0389200; 129: gvhs vhs00236; 153: gvs01 vhs00110; 164–65: glva01 lva00171; 196: g3842a cw0250100

Courtesy of Prints & Photographs, Library of Congress:
16: LC-DIG-stereo-1s02416 (hand colored); 20t: LC-DIG-ppmsca-37137; 21, 198, 199, 204tl: LC-DIG-cwpb-04351; 24: LC-DIG-ppmsca-19469; 26tl: LC-DIG-cwpb-06941; 26br: LC-DIG-cwpb-05008; 27: LC-DIG-cwpb-05210; 26–27 (background): LC-DIG-ppmsca-31813; 28: LC-DIG-cwpb-04402; 29: LC-USZ62-1625; 30tr: LC-DIG-cwpb-05210; 31: LC-DIG-cwpb-05341; 32: LC-DIG-cwpb-05989; 33: LC-DIG-cwpbh-00682; 32–33 (background): LC-DIG-ppmsca-2136; 34tl: LC-DIG-cwpb-06205; 34br: LC-DIG-cwpb-05983; 35tr: LC-DIG-cwpb-05368; 35bl: LC-DIG-cwpb-06979; 37tl: LC-B8184-10086; 37br: LC-B8184-10527; 38br: LC-B8184-10692; 39: LC-B8184-10339; 40tl: LC-B8184-10582; 40br: LC-B8184-10430; 40–41 (background): LC-DIG-pga-01158; 41bl: LC-B8184-10037; 41tr: LC-B8184-10038; 42t: LC-B8184-10178; 42b: LC-B8184-10374; 43: LC-B8184-10575; 46–47 (background), 56, 57, 66b: LC-DIG-cwpb-04294; 48, 66tl: LC-DIG-cwpb-00737; 49, 50–51, 67t: LC-DIG-cwpb-01005; 52, 53, 66tr: LC-DIG-cwpb-00747; 54: LC-DIG-cwpb-00821; 55: LC-DIG-cwpb-02011; 58: LC-DIG-cwpb-03351; 59: LC-DIG-cwpb-01926; 60, 61, 67br: LC-DIG-cwpb-02004; 62: LC-DIG-cwpb-00468; 63: LC-DIG-cwpb-01930; 64, 67bl: LC-DIG-cwpb-04324; 68–69, 75: LC-DIG-cwpb-01402; 71, 145tl: LC-DIG-cwpb-01663; 18, 72: LC-DIG-cwpb-01553; 73: LC-DIG-cwpb-00755; 74: LC-DIG-cwpb-00955; 22–23, 76, 77: LC-DIG-cwpb-01590; 78: LC-DIG-cwpb-01010; 79: LC-DIG-cwpb-00164; 80, 81: LC-DIG-cwpb-01579; 82, 82–83b, 145bl: LC-DIG-cwpb-03792; 83t: LC-DIG-cwpb-01024; 82–83 (background): LC-DIG-ppmsca-21470; 84: LC-DIG-cwpb-01604; 85: LC-DIG-cwpb-01848; 86, 87: LC-DIG-cwpb-01702; 16t, 16b, 88: LC-DIG-cwpb-01063; 89: LC-DIG-cwpb-00205; 20b: 90: LC-DIG-cwpb-04335; 91: LC-DIG-cwpb-02136; 92: LC-DIG-cwpb-03974; 93: LC-DIG-cwpb-01652; 94: LC-DIG-cwpb-03803; 96: LC-DIG-cwpb-00074; 96 (background): LC-DIG-ppmsca-20442; 97: LC-DIG-cwpb-01660; 98t: LC-DIG-cwpb-00815; 98b: LC-DIG-cwpb-03984; 99: LC-DIG-cwpb-03915; 2–3, 100: LC-DIG-cwpb-04015; 101: LC-DIG-cwpb-03686; 102: LC-DIG-cwpb-01140; 6–7, 103: LC-DIG-cwpb-04333; 104, 105: LC-DIG-cwpb-02110; 106, 144tl: LC-DIG-cwpb-03404; 107, 144bl: LC-DIG-cwpb-03628; 108: LC-DIG-cwpb-01564; 15, 109: LC-DIG-cwpb-01829; 110: LC-DIG-cwpb-02163; 111: LC-DIG-cwpb-03816; 112t: LC-DIG-cwpb-02195; 112b: LC-DIG-cwpb-02209; 113, 144br: LC-DIG-cwpb-02221; 114, 115: LC-DIG-cwpb-01196; 116, 117: LC-DIG-cwpb-00348; 118, 119: LC-DIG-cwpb-01813; 120: LC-DIG-cwpb-04407; 121: LC-DIG-cwpb-03795; 122–123:

LC-DIG-cwpb-03857; 124, 145tr: LC-DIG-cwpb-03882; 125tl: LC-DIG-cwpb-03714; 125br: LC-DIG-cwpb-02773; 126: LC-DIG-cwpb-03159; 127: LC-DIG-cwpb-02759; 128tl: LC-DIG-cwpb-02860; 128br: LC-DIG-cwpb-03108; 129tl: LC-DIG-cwpb-01319; 129br: LC-DIG-cwpb-01953; 130: LC-DIG-cwpb-04113; 131: LC-DIG-cwpb-04358; 19, 132–33: LC-DIG-cwpb-04022; 133: LC-DIG-cwpb-02955; 134, 145br: LC-DIG-cwpb-01897; 135tr: LC-DIG-cwpb-01854; 135bl: LC-DIG-cwpb-01964; 136: LC-DIG-cwpb-04246; 137: LC-DIG-cwpb-02055; 138: LC-DIG-cwpb-03518; 140: LC-DIG-cwpb-03950; 142: LC-DIG-cwpb-06586; 146–47 (background), 166,167: LC-DIG-cwpb-02752; 150: LC-DIG-cwpb-00133; 151: LC-DIG-cwpb-01053; 152: LC-DIG-cwpb-01057; 153: LC-DIG-cwpb-01061; 152–53 (background): LC-DIG-pga-01840; 154, 174b: LC-DIG-cwpb-04727; 156, 174tr: LC-DIG-cwpb-02987; 157tr: LC-DIG-cwpb-01345; 157bl: LC-DIG-cwpb-00636; 158: LC-DIG-cwpb-01368; 159: LC-DIG-cwpb-04350; 160, 161, 175tl: LC-DIG-cwpb-02197; 162–163: LC-DIG-cwpb-03851; 164: LC-DIG-cwpb-01513; 165: LC-DIG-cwpb-00015; 168: LC-DIG-cwpb-00025; 169, 175tr: LC-DIG-cwpb-02580; 170: LC-DIG-cwpb-02976; 172: LC-DIG-cwpb-00708; 173, 175bl: LC-DIG-cwpb-03515; 176–77, 182: LC-DIG-cwpb-02657; 178–79, 191t: LC-DIG-cwpb-00302; 180, 191bl: LC-DIG-cwpb-02532; 181, 190tl: LC-DIG-cwpb-02705; 183, 190tr: LC-DIG-cwpb-00408; 184, 185, 190b: LC-DIG-cwpb-03049 ; 186, 187: LC-DIG-cwpb-02364; 188: LC-DIG-cwpb-02679; 189, 191bl: LC-DIG-cwpb-02675; 192–93, 200–201, 204tr: LC-DIG-cwpb-04352; 194, 195, 205:LC-DIG-cwpb-04326; 197, 204bl: LC-DIG-cwpb-04339; 202–3, 204bl: LC-DIG-cwpb-07639; 206–7, 224, 225: LC-DIG-cwpb-03928; 208, 209, 227tr: LC-DIG-cwpb-00240; 210: LC-DIG-cwpb-00831; 211, 227bl: LC-DIG-cwpb-00864; 212, 226b: LC-DIG-cwpb-04337; 213: LC-DIG-cwpb-00849; 214, 226tr: LC-DIG-cwpb-00877; 215: LC-DIG-cwpb-00916; 216, 217, 227tl: LC-DIG-cwpb-01843; 218, 226tl: LC-DIG-cwpb-01186; 219: LC-DIG-cwpb-01187; 220: LC-DIG-cwpb-01887; 221: LC-DIG-cwpb-01885; 222: LC-DIG-cwpb-02539; 223, 227br: LC-DIG-cwpb-02550; 228–29, 240–41, 245: LC-DIG-cwpb-02803; 230–31, 242: LC-DIG-cwpb-02464; 232, 232–33 (background). 243bl: LC-DIG-cwpb-03957; 233, 243br: LC-DIG-cwpb-04406; 234–35, 235, 243tr: LC-DIG-cwpb-04202; 236: LC-DIG-cwpb-02960; 237t: LC-DIG-cwpbh-03254; 237b: LC-USZC4-1834; 238, 238–39, 243tl: LC-DIG-cwpb-03813

Courtesy the National Archives, Washington, D.C.:
25: 111-B-4146; 30bl: 111-B-2520; 36: 111-B-1074; 1, 28–29 (background), 70, 144tr: 121-BA-914A; 141: 111-B-256; 149, 174tl: 77-HL-99-1

A NOTE ON THE FINE ART PRINT

The vellum envelope at the back of *The Civil War in Color* contains a photographic fine art print of "Powder monkey by gun of USS *New Hampshire* off Charleston, S.C.," c. 1864, colorized by John Guntzelman. The print is reproduced on 200 gsm Garda Pat 13 Kiara paper, and is printed stochastically by 1010 Printing International Ltd, in China. The image is also reproduced on page 173 of this book.